Programming for People
with Special Needs

Programming for People with Special Needs

A Guide for Museums and Historic Sites

Katie Stringer

ROWMAN & LITTLEFIELD
Lanham • Boulder • New York • London

Published by Rowman & Littlefield
A wholly owned subsidiary of The Rowman & Littlefield Publishing Group, Inc.
4501 Forbes Boulevard, Suite 200, Lanham, Maryland 20706
www.rowman.com

16 Carlisle Street, London W1D 3BT, United Kingdom

British Library Cataloguing in Publication Information Available

Library of Congress Cataloging-in-Publication Data

Stringer, Katie, 1986–
Programming for people with special needs : a guide for museums and historic sites / Katie Stringer.
pages cm. — (American Association for State and Local History Book Series)
Includes bibliographical references and index.
ISBN 978-1-4422-2760-6 (cloth : alk. paper)—ISBN 978-1-4422-2761-3 (pbk. : alk. paper)—ISBN
978-1-4422-2765-1 (electronic : alk. paper)
1. Museums and people with disabilities. 2. Learning disabled. 3. Museum buildings—Barrier-free
design. 4. Museums and people with disabilities—United States. 5. Learning disabled—United
States. 6. Museum buildings—Barrier-free design—United States. I. Title.
AM160.S77 2014
069'.17—dc23
2014008850

∞™ The paper used in this publication meets the minimum requirements of American
National Standard for Information Sciences Permanence of Paper for Printed Library
Materials, ANSI/NISO Z39.48-1992.

Printed in the United States of America

This work is dedicated to my father.
Thank you for inspiring my work, always supporting my dreams, and believing that they could come true.

Contents

Acknowledgments

I would like to thank my academic advisers and especially Dr. Carroll Van West for his editing skills through many drafts and for motivating me to finish this manuscript in its original form. Dr. Robert Connolly from the University of Memphis helped me become the museum professional that I am today through program course work and experiential opportunities in the Memphis community, and his mentorship continues to inspire and encourage me.

The wonderful museum professionals in New York City who took time to speak with me jump-started this process, and their advice was invaluable to my research. Additionally, the students and teachers who participated in surveys and field studies were integral to this body of work, and I am grateful for their time and input.

My delightful friends at the Historic Sam Davis Home and Museum in Smyrna, Tennessee—Meredith Baughman, Rebecca Key Duke, Madelyne Rush, Shirley Carter, and the rest of the staff—were so supportive and helpful throughout the case study and beyond.

My granddad, Charles Stringer, first instilled in me a love and respect of history, and I thank him for his influence and support. I wish to thank my fantastic parents, Mark and Brenda, for their enduring love and their encouragement of my educational dreams from the first time that I visited a historical museum; I love you both! My sweet Charles deserves the highest accolades for abiding with me and always giving me the perfect pep talk. He continues to love and support me, and he never lets me give up. I love you!

Preface

The purpose of this manual is to assist museums and historic sites in the process of creating inclusive sites of education and well-being for all visitors, especially those with disabilities or special needs. The book distills the successes and failures of other museums in order to offer ideas and support to museum professionals who want to create programs for all audiences. The seven key elements of effective programs that I developed from a case study provide the framework for others to adapt existing programs for visitors with special needs.

Programming for People with Special Needs: A Guide for Museums and Historic Sites is unique because it covers education and inclusion for those with intellectual disabilities and learning disability, which goes beyond the regular "fixes" of compliance with the Americans with Disabilities Act for those with physical disabilities. The challenges that small museums and historic sites face when trying to create truly inclusive experiences are discussed along with suggestions for making successful programs.

This book is aimed at museum educators and administrators as well as those interested in informal education. It is essential that all museum and historic site professionals, especially educators or administrators, have an understanding of access for visitors. Students of museum studies or public history as well as individuals interested in informal education and scholars interested in disability history or studies may also find information that benefits them.

The manual opens with a discussion of the history of museums as educational centers and includes a brief history of disability in the United States, including advocacy and laws related to accessibility. The book also includes a chapter on etiquette that museum employees should refer to when working with visitors who have disabilities. I investigate sensitivity and awareness training for all museum staff and offer suggestions for training and interactions with visitors.

Universal design and inclusiveness of all visitors to museums is another attribute of the book. Chapter 3 explains what universal design is and how museums and historic sites can benefit from implementing programs, exhibits, and spaces that adhere to universal design standards.

Chapter 4 reviews model programs, such as the "Meet Me" program at the Museum of Modern Art and the programs for children with autism at the Transit Museum in Brooklyn. Details about the programs and ways to adapt those programs for various audiences are explored.

Chapter 5 includes a case study of best practices for creating museum programs for all visitors, especially those with special needs. Central to the research is a case study at a local historic site with a special education class. This study focuses on a historic house museum in Smyrna, Tennessee, giving contrast to the larger metropolitan museum programs reviewed in chapter 4. From this case study, I present a model of best practices for museums to use in developing programming and welcoming an underserved population to their organization. The book ends with suggestions for museum professionals to make their own museums universally designed and accessible for audiences with special needs.

Effective public history dialogue depends on all voices having adequate access to interpretation and experience set in historical or cultural environments. Creative educational programming and implementation of universal design can offer all learners an impactful encounter at a museum or a historic site. From a small town in Tennessee to the largest museums in New York City, accessible education has been realized; let your site or museum be the next to fulfill this objective.

Chapter One

Museums, Education, and Accessibility

People value history in different ways and for different reasons. They engage with history writing, either as authors, as consumers, or as students, to understand their own past and heritage, to learn about other cultures and peoples, or sometimes to try to learn from the past to inform the future. The twenty-first century is a world of instant communication yet personal disconnections; people find that history, presented in film, in print, or in a re-created production, may allow them to see connections and themes among seemingly disparate groups of people, nations, and cultures.

This search for connections and audience is familiar territory for all histo rians and museum professionals in particular. They bring context to the particular and connect what is local to broader regional, national, or even international themes. In the best situations, they make sense out of what can be the nonsense of local heritage.

THE ROLE OF MUSEUMS AS CENTERS FOR EDUCATION

Museums and historic sites have long been considered places of public education in various forms. Early institutions, however, served a limited public. Considered to be the first "modern" museum, the Ashmolean Museum in England opened at Oxford University in 1683; it is generally thought to be the first museum established by a public body for the public benefit.[1] Elias Ashmole donated his collections to the university in 1677. The collection contained natural history specimens, coins, books, and art and was essentially a "cabinet of curiosities."[2] These collections represent those things that were foreign and intriguing to Oxford students, faculty, and residents and thus could be classified as one of the most well-known cabinets of curiosities.

Less than a century after the establishment of the Ashmolean Museum, the British Museum opened in London in 1759, and a generation later, the Louvre opened in Paris. The audiences of both institutions were much broader than that of their predecessors, and their respective governments opened the museums and used them to display private and royal collections.[3]

Developers of museums in early America could not depend on government patronage; rather, they marketed their institutions to a much larger public by the scope and nature of their collections. Artist, inventor, and entrepreneur Charles Willson Peale opened the first major "museum" in Philadelphia in 1794. In a broadside distributed to the American Philosophical Society and other prominent social figures of Philadelphia, Peale emphasized that his museum would both collect and exhibit publicly a wide range of artifacts, focusing on natural history and art but including historical items as well. His museum was a for-profit enterprise. To keep the doors open, he depended on attractions that ensured repeat customers.[4] Peale's museum struggled, and eventually entertainment broker P. T. Barnum bought most of the collection.[5] When that museum burned in 1865, few complained. Once Barnum's American Museum was closed because of the fire, Edwin Lawrence Godkin called for a new museum that would do justice to that title. He said, "It is in behalf of all classes of the community, except that vicious ad degraded one by which the late 'American Museum' was largely monopolized, that we ask the community for a building and for collections that shall be worthy of the name so sadly misapplied."[6] He wished that the new great New York City museum would be worthy of the name. With the creation of the Metropolitan Museum of Art in 1870, Godkin and other New York elites got their wish.[7]

Museums soon became recognized as places of research and higher education. Herman August Hagen, a professor at the Museum of Comparative Zoology at Harvard University, called for separating exhibit and research collections, leading to the establishment of modern museum practices.[8] Hagan brought an academic rigor to the Victorian debate about museums in the United States. He wanted museums to serve as institutions for public learning rather than repositories for scholars and the elite. He insisted that museums should "show how museums intended to advance knowledge, namely, collections for public instruction, can be made and arranged so as to be best fitted for their purpose."[9]

In 1883, British reformer Stanley W. Jevons echoed Hagan's call for museums to embrace an educational mission. But Jevons also wondered if the public could accept the diversity, chronological range, and ancient meanings of most museum collections. Museum guides or interpreters became one of Jevons's solutions.[10]

Luigi Palma di Cesnola was the first director of the Metropolitan Museum of Art in New York City. In 1887, he asserted that all museums had public value, "whether it be one to display the products of art and industry, the relics of human antiquity, the remnants of palaeozoic life, the crystallized beauties of the mineral kingdom, or the gathered specimens from the realm of organized nature." He asserted that museums should be seen not as "an index of the money-spending power of this or that individual or association" but rather as an "object-library" where visitors can observe and study but cannot remove or check out the items. This object-library would educate the general public through objects in such a way that the visitors would leave with new ideas and knowledge. By visiting a museum, the visitor would "no longer be left to the haziness and impracticability that too often cling to mere book learning."[11]

John Edward Gray of the British Museum popularized the concept of the "New Museum" in the late nineteenth century. This new concept of museums focuses on education of the public in exhibition spaces that are separate from research collections.[12]

In 1908, Frederic A. Lucas, the director of the Brooklyn Museum and later the American Museum of Natural History in New York City, reaffirmed the importance of education in an address to the Staten Island Association of Arts and Sciences. His essay "Purpose and Aims of Modern Museums" pointed to a range of museum directors and curators who believed that education was a museum's primary mission. Lucas believed that the "museum of today is a great deal more than a place where objects are merely preserved, it is an educational institution on a large scale, whose language may be understood by all, an ever open book whose pages appeal not only to the scholar but even to the man who cannot read." Lucas believed that museums must involve the visitors in the work, methods, and results to gain their interest and support. He concluded, "Over and beyond these things are the educational opportunities offered to everyone and, after all, love of knowledge is the supreme test of civilization."[13]

John Cotton Dana built on the insistence for museum education. The founder and first director of the Newark Museum in New Jersey, Dana was a prolific writer who focused on museum philosophy and purpose. As historian Edward P. Alexander argues, Dana merged the concept of museum with community service. He built a tradition, adopted by many, that a museum was "conducted for the good of the whole community."[14] Dana was a revolutionary in the field of public education and the institutions that supplement general education. For instance, he encouraged the opening of stacks in the library so that scholars could search the books themselves rather than being restricted by the librarian. He also included objects in his library for the public to view as they would in a museum. Dana wanted to reenergize American museums, which he saw as isolated and distant repositories, with what is now called object-centered education programming.

Object-centered education is at the forefront of most modern museum education initiatives. The American Association of Museums' *Riches, Rivals, and Radicals: 100 Years of Museums* (2006) pinpointed education as a primary museum goal. The study's author, Marjorie Schwartz, concluded that museums today are places of "exchange, encounter, and education," though in the past they were little more than repositories for objects of wealthy donors. Schwartz insisted that museums "collect, preserve, display, interpret, and educate for the public good" and offer the opportunity to learn and be informed.[15] The International Council of Museums agrees with this approach. It defined a museum as a

> non-profit, permanent institution in the service of society and its development, open to the public, which acquires, conserves, researches, communicates and exhibits the tangible and intangible heritage of humanity and its environment for the purposes of education, study and enjoyment.[16]

The definition includes society, the public, and education in addition to collections and conservation, a significant shift in attitude and practice.

Despite their significance, museum education departments still struggle to gain respect and are often isolated, do not have high esteem in the museum hierarchy, and lead a frustrating battle for the rights of their visitors.[17] The transformation from a place of research and knowledge for elite scholars to a place of learning for all audiences will require the assistance of the entire museum, not just the educational department.

Today, museum educators find that a reliance on Common Core Standards programs helps in their fight to stay relevant and funded.[18] Educators also have recently combated the fad of standards-based curricula by linking programs to the specific state curriculum of each grade level.[19] If a program can be marketed to teachers as comprising several of the check marks required for students in their tests, teachers will be more inclined to bring the students, thus increasing visitor numbers and revenue at the museum. They hope a similar strategy will drive teachers in Common Core Standards programs to visit museums since the collections are primary sources.

Compared to the mind-numbing standardization of tests and test preparation, museum learning in galleries and exhibits is informal and creative. This casual style of teaching and learning could attract students and teachers to the museum as a release from the standardized test atmosphere of schools.[20] Museum educational programs are ideally experimental and involve hands-on aspects that encourage creativity.[21] This latter trait underscores the museum's potential for audiences with intellectual disabilities and other cognitive and developmental disabilities of all ages.

Museums and historic sites are key parts of the public history world. Museums as forums for dialogue mean that even small professional institutions have education programs for the public. Many museums offer programs that are specifically catered to certain groups, or they have specialized lectures and hands-on programs for students to learn more about a specific aspect of history that the historic site or museum provides.

Creating education programs for children is challenging for any instructor. The ways that schoolchildren understand and learn about the past are variable. Elaine Davis, in *How Students Understand the Past*, explains that, to understand how to teach history, one must also know how the past is constructed in the minds of individuals who are shaped in turn by their age, culture, ethnicity, and other factors.[22] Davis argues that historical knowledge is constructed in two ways: narrative understanding and logical-scientific understanding. The former is perhaps the most important to the processing of this new information in students' minds, while the latter is generally the kind of learning that takes place in the classroom.

To stimulate informal learning, Davis argues for active engagement, and objects such as artifacts or replicas help a learner connect to the past on a personal level. By using interactive and object-based learning, students are more engaged and connected in studies of the past.[23] This is an essential component of creating programs for all visitors, and adaptations will result in effective programs for anyone who visits.

DISABILITY RIGHTS AND AWARENESS

The 1960 election of John F. Kennedy as president of the United States elevated disability rights to the forefront of the government. Kennedy's sister Rosemary was born with an intellectual disability, and the Kennedy administration actively worked to support those with disabilities. In 1961, Kennedy created the President's Panel on Mental Retardation to set goals, planning services, and funding for research and developmental projects.

In 1962, educator Samuel Kirk created the term "learning disabilities," which helped target those whose disabilities had not previously been classified as a disability. In his book *Educating Exceptional Children* (1962), he claimed that the term

> refers to a retardation, disorder, or delayed development in one or more of the processes of speech, language, reading, writing, arithmetic, or other school subject resulting from a psychological handicap caused by a possible cerebral dysfunction and/or emotional or behavioral disturbances. It is not the result of mental retardation, sensory deprivation, or cultural and instructional factors.[24]

This definition separated those with learning difficulties from those with mental retardation and thus influenced the way that children were taught in special education classes and in their mainstream counterparts.

In a message to Congress in 1962, Kennedy emphasized the importance of education of those with disabilities:

> Another long-standing national concern has been the provision of specially trained teachers to meet the educational needs of children afflicted with physical and mental disabilities. . . . [I] recommend broadening the basic program to include assistance for the special training needed to help all our children afflicted with the entire range of physical and mental handicaps. [25]

The President's Panel on Mental Retardation presented over 100 recommendations to Kennedy to create a better educational environment for people with disabilities in the year after their formation. [26] One year after the address to Congress on education, on February 5, 1963, in the "Special Message to the Congress on Mental Illness and Mental Retardation," Kennedy outlined his plan for the education of individuals with mental retardation. The plan included new programs for maternity and prenatal care, a move away from institutions that had become custodial to instructional agencies, and an increase in special education, training, and rehabilitation. [27] The lasting effect of this committee was President Lyndon B. Johnson's creation in 1966 of the President's Committee for People with Intellectual Disabilities, which is still in existence today.

In November 1975, President Gerald Ford signed Public Law 94-142, the Education for All Handicapped Children Act. This law made it possible for all children with disabilities to integrate more effectively into public schools and society. PL 94-142 guaranteed a free, appropriate public education to each child with a disability in every state and locality across the country. Today, PL 94-142 is still in existence and is known as the Individuals with Disabilities Education Act (IDEA), serving children from birth to age twenty-one. [28]

The Americans with Disabilities Act (ADA) of 1990 was the first major legislation that provided a promise of equality to all people with disabilities. However, Arlene Mayerson observed in her 1992 article "The History of the ADA: A Movement Perspective" that the ADA did not begin with the congressional legislation of 1990; it began much earlier with the people and communities that fought against discrimination. [29] Legally, the shift toward disability equality began in 1973 when Congress passed Section 505 of the Rehabilitation Act, which banned discrimination based on disability for the receiving of federal funds. Following this action, the disability civil rights movement gained momentum, and in 1988, the ADA was first brought forward to Congress for consideration. In 1990, Congress passed the act, which gave rights to people with disabilities that had previously not been guaranteed by federal law. Essentially, the law protected against disability discrimination in employment, public services, public accommodation and services operated by private entities, transportation, and telecommunications.

This study uses the term "intellectual disability" to refer to mental disability, such as mental retardation or cognitive delay, in accordance with Rosa's Law, or Public Law 111-256. Rosa's Law was signed by President Barack Obama on October 5, 2010. The law serves to "change references in Federal law to mental retardation to references to an intellectual disability."[30]

EARLY EXHIBITIONS OF PEOPLE WITH DISABILITIES

From the popular Coney Island amusement area in New York City to traveling circuses and sideshows, exhibits that featured people with physical differences were some of the most prevalent attractions of the nineteenth and early twentieth centuries. Dime museums and national exhibitions up to the mid-twentieth century often featured humans who were considered different for the public to view and experience. The exhibition of people in these shows was sometimes voluntary, but most often were acts of desperation from people whom the mass culture considered to be "freaks." The place of those individuals with disabilities, especially those with intellectual disabilities, is an important piece of the past that informs present displays and exhibits, museum policies, and popular attitudes. Even today, modern sideshows are available to the public in various forums.

For over 100 years, entrepreneurs organized exhibitions of people with physical, mental, and behavioral disabilities or impairments to attract the public and generate a profit.[31] Many times, they advertised exhibitions as educational and scientific activities.[32] Barnum's museum and others like it became known as dime museums. They often housed gaffes or fake objects and people and were little more than a circus or carnival sideshow exhibit. While people likely did not conflate museums with sideshows, the sideshows were generally billed as educational events and opportunities, and the sideshow did grow out of the dime museum tradition.

The dime museum of nineteenth-century America allowed the general population to see "dioramas, panoramas, georamas, cosmoramas, paintings, relics, freaks, stuffed animals, menageries, waxworks, and theatrical performance."[33] The museums served as escapes for Victorian Americans.[34] For many, the word "museum" thus became irrevocably associated with the weird, strange, and unknown.[35] Exhibitions such as the blockbuster *Bodies* exhibit and the plethora of Ripley's Believe It or Not Odditoriums in every major tourist town in America continue to suggest sideshow and exploitative aspects of museums.

Here is where I wish to address both the museum professional's desire to reach as broad of an audience as possible[36] and the historical legacy of past discrimination, with a particular focus on people with intellectual disabilities and other related cognitive and developmental disabilities.[37]

Museums and historic sites as forums for dialogue and engagement fail when they are designed and structured to keep groups at arm's length due to race, class, ethnicity, or disability. There has been a marked exclusion of people with intellectual disability in museums, even today. In many cases, people with disabilities are rarely part of the audience of history museums or historical sites.

ACCESSIBILITY AT MUSEUMS AND HISTORIC SITES

Historic sites have the challenge of accessibility; rarely in the past were structures or spaces designed with special needs in mind. Yet allowing difficulty in movement to be the factor separating museum educators from potential audiences undercuts the museum's role in public dialogue, and it is not legal to do so.

With the passage of the ADA in 1990, museums and all public spaces were required to become accessible to all populations. ADA guidelines state, "The following private entities are considered public accommodations for purposes of this subchapter, if the operations of such entities affect commerce . . . (H) a museum, library, gallery, or other place of public display or collection." Additionally, Section 12182 explains that

> no individual shall be discriminated against on the basis of disability in the full and equal enjoyment of the goods, services, facilities, privileges, advantages, or accommodations of any place of public accommodation by any person who owns, leases (or leases to), or operates a place of public accommodation.[38]

The ADA has opened the door to new audiences who may not otherwise have had the opportunity to visit these museums or historic sites.

Approximately 17,500 museums across the United States operated at the time that the department published the article, and all of those museums had legal obligations to provide accessibility. Private museums are covered under ADA Title III, and public institutions are covered under ADA Title II; museums that receive federal funding are covered by Section 504 of the Rehabilitation Act. For compliance, the U.S. Department of Justice provides many tips for museums on its website, including information about accessible entrances, routes throughout the museum, and accessibility in program offerings by the museum. Many of these accommodations apply to people who use mobility devices or are sight and/or hearing impaired.[39]

Benefits to creating barrier-free and accessible programs are myriad; according to the Department of Justice, accessibility can include over 50 million people with disabilities in America. More than 20 million families have a member with a disability, and millions of baby boomers become disabled with age.[40]

The Association of Science-Technology Centers also provides a useful resource for museums' legal obligations for accessible practices.[41] The guide mentions accommodations for barrier-free education and access, but it does not address accessibility for people with intellectual disabilities or learning disabilities as much. Museum officials wonder what they should do in the post-ADA world to go beyond the legal obligations to serve their entire community. There are many museums in the United States and abroad that are working toward inclusion of all people with disabilities at their museum or historic site.

Accessibility at historic house museums creates individual issues that are recognized by the Department of Justice on the web page "ADA Requirements for Small Towns." The document provides an example of a historic house museum, its challenges, and how those challenges were overcome. The example is of an actual two-story historic house museum from 1885 that provides exhibition and instructional programs for the public. An evaluation determines that the house is not accessible, but the town decides that moving museum programs to other accessible locations would not be possible because the historic house is a critical part of the programs. Managers of the house museum instead provided access to the first floor of the historic house in compliance with ADA standards and historic preservation requirements. The state's historic preservation office determined that creating accessible features for the second floor of the house would threaten the features and historic significance of the house. Rather than destroying the historical integrity of the house, the museum managers located all programs on the first floor of the house, and experiences of the second floor were made available through photos and video.[42] These approaches are typical, but as the following chapters will demonstrate, there are more options for historic house museums and small museums.

In *Running a Museum: A Practical Handbook*, Vicky Woollard asks, "What is access?" She defines museum access as

> giving the visitor the opportunity to use facilities and services, view displays, attend lectures, research and study the collections, and to meet staff. This does not only mean physical access, but also includes access at the appropriate intellectual level that is free from social and cultural prejudice.[43]

Woollard cites Article 27 of the United Nations Universal Declaration of Human Rights 1948, which states, "Everyone has the right freely to participate in the cultural life of the community, to enjoy the arts and to share in scientific advancement and its benefits."[44] Then she asserts that museums and the programs and exhibits that they offer fall under the right to participation in cultural life, and therefore, there should be no discrimination against age, sex, religious or cultural beliefs, disabilities, or sexual orientation at these places.[45]

The scholarship on "what is access" over the past twenty years emphasized the challenge to public historians at museums and historic sites. All audiences must be served, and all audiences may benefit from well-crafted, inclusive narratives, be they the guided site tour or the exhibit hall. To become truly inclusive museums, administrators must devise ways to reach all audiences. Removing physical barriers to access through universal design principles would meet the ADA's requirements. Just as important is to create a greater reliance on direct experience and hands-on learning to engage those with intellectual disabilities with the museum collections and setting.

CONCLUSION

This manual aims to create effective examples and guidelines for creating programming for this targeted group. The book then explores how the potential of universal design concepts may combine with object-centered learning to create museum and historic site educational initiatives that are effective for students and nonprofit organizations.

Creating these programs will help visitors see the world as an interconnected, diverse place where all are welcomed to interact and engage with various populations within their community. It is of utmost importance to develop these programs in league with the community that the curriculum will serve and with educators in the special education field.

The goal of this book is not only to analyze these issues but also to offer potential solutions in a close study of educational programming and the resultant public dialogue from sites in the major museum hubs of New York City and Washington, DC, and also smaller historic sites representative of the low-budget and understaffed sites that are common in every town and region. Through analysis of existing programs and case studies, I produce guidelines and a model for other museums and sites of all sizes and budgets to adapt to create better programming for all visitors.

NOTES

1. Geoffrey Lewis, "The Role of Museums and the Professional Code of Ethics," in *Running a Museum: A Practical Handbook*, ed. International Council of Museums (Paris: International Council of Museums, 2010), 2.
2. Hugh H. Genoways and Mary Anne Andrei, eds., *Museum Origins: Readings in Early Museum History and Philosophy* (Walnut Creek, CA: Left Coast Press, 2008), 19, 21.
3. Lewis, "The Role of Museums and the Professional Code of Ethics," 3.
4. Genoways and Andrei, *Museum Origins*, 23.

5. More comprehensive studies of Peale's museum are available in Sarah Lynn Davis, "What Happened to Baltimore's Peale Museum? An Examination into Urban History Museums" (master's thesis, University of Maryland, Baltimore County, 2008); Edward P. Alexander, *Museum Masters: Their Museums and Their Influence* (Nashville: American Association for State and Local History, 1983), 43–78; Charles C. Sellers, *Mr. Peale's Museum: Charles Wilson Peale and the First Popular Museum of Natural Science and Art* (New York: Norton, 1980); and Gary Kulik, "Designing the Past: History-Museum Exhibitions from Peale to the Present," in *History Museums in the United States: A Critical Assessment*, ed. Warren Leon and Roy Rosenweig (Urbana: University of Illinois Press, 1989).

6. Edwin L. Godkin, "A Word about Museums," *The Nation*, July 27, 1865, 113–14.

7. Edward Porter Alexander and Mary Alexander, *Museums in Motion: An Introduction to the History and Functions of Museums* (New York: AltaMira Press, 2008), 31–32.

8. Genoways and Andrei, *Museum Origins*, 39.

9. Herman August Hagen, "The History of the Origin and Development of Museums," *American Naturalist* 10 (1876): 80–89.

10. Stanley W. Jevons, "The Use and Abuse of Museums," in *Methods of Social Reform and Other Papers* (London: Macmillan, 1883).

11. Luigi Palma di Cesnola, *An Address on the Practical Value of the American Museum* (Troy, NY: Stowell Printing House, 1887), 1.

12. Genoways and Andrei, *Museum Origins*, 97.

13. Frederic A. Lucas, "Purpose and Aims of Modern Museums," in *Proceedings—Staten Island Institute of Arts and Sciences*, vol. 2, ed. Philip Dowell, Arthur Hollick, and William T. Davis (Lancaster, PA: New Era Printing Company, 1910), 119.

14. Alexander, *Museum Masters*, 405.

15. Marjorie Schwartz, *Riches, Rivals, and Radicals: 100 Years of Museums* (Washington, DC: American Association of Museums, 2006), 2, 3.

16. International Council of Museums, "Museum Definition," http://icom.museum/the-vision/museum-definition (accessed August 6, 2013).

17. Claudia Haas, "Families and Children Challenging Museums," in *The Manual of Museum Learning*, ed. Barry Lord (Lanham, MD: AltaMira Press, 2007), 50.

18. See the extensive discussion and materials at Common Core State Standards Initiative at http://www.corestandards.org (accessed April 2, 2013).

19. Howard Gardner, *The Unschooled Mind: How Children Think and How Schools Should Teach* (New York: Basic Books, 1991), 79.

20. Gardner, *Unschooled Mind*, 97.

21. Gardner, *Unschooled Mind*, 97.

22. Elaine Davis, *How Students Understand the Past: From Theory to Practice* (Walnut Creek, CA: AltaMira Press, 2005), 17.

23. Davis, *How Students Understand the Past*, 119.

24. Samuel Kirk, *Educating Exceptional Children* (Boston: Houghton Mifflin, 1962), 263.

25. John F. Kennedy, "Special Message to the Congress on Education," February 6, 1962, *The American Presidency Project*, ed. Gerhard Peters and John T. Woolley, http://www.presidency.ucsb.edu/ws/?pid=8858 (accessed April 2, 2013). See also Edward Shorter, *The Kennedy Family and the Story of Mental Retardation* (Philadelphia: Temple University Press, 2000).

26. John F. Kennedy Presidential Library, "JFK and People with Intellectual Disabilities," http://www.jfklibrary.org/JFK/JFK-in-History/JFK-and-People-with-Intellectual-Disabilities.aspx (accessed April 2, 2013).

27. John F. Kennedy, "Special Message to the Congress on Mental Illness and Mental Retardation," February 5, 1963, in *The American Presidency Project*, ed. Gerhard Peters and John T. Woolley, http://www.presidency.ucsb.edu/ws/?pid=9546 (accessed April 2, 2013).

28. Office of Special Education Programs, *Twenty-Five Years of Progress in Educating Children with Disabilities through IDEA* (Washington, DC: U.S. Department of Education, 2007).

29. Arlene Mayerson, "The History of the ADA: A Movement Perspective," *Disability Rights Education and Defense Fund*, 1992, http://dredf.org/publications/ada_history.shtml (accessed January 10, 2013).

30. Rosa's Law, Public Law 111-256, 111th Cong., 2nd sess. (October 5, 2010).

31. People with physical disabilities or anomalies are generally called "born different" peoples, unlike those who are "made freaks" by swallowing swords or nailing objects into their heads. Today's freak shows consist mainly of people who are "made freaks" who do dangerous tricks or have a rare talents, though there are some instances of "born differents" still today.

32. Godkin, "A Word about Museums," 113–14.

33. Andrea Stulman Dennett, *Weird and Wonderful: The Dime Museum in America* (New York: New York University Press, 1997), 5.

34. Dennett, *Weird and Wonderful*, 7.

35. More information about the rise and impact of dime museums and the entertainment industry as a whole is available in Dennett, *Weird and Wonderful*; John Kasson, *Amusing the Million: Coney Island at the Turn of the Century* (New York: Hill and Wang, 1978); Genoways and Andrei, *Museum Origins*; Sellers, *Mr. Peale's Museum*; and Kulik, "Designing the Past," 3–37.

36. International Council of Museums, *Running a Museum*, 105; Harpers Ferry Center Accessibility Task Force, *Special Populations: Programmatic Accessibility Guidelines* (Harpers Ferry, WV: National Park Service, June 1999), 1.

37. The terminology and definitions related to medical conditions and special education vary throughout time and across disciplines. The terms "mental retardation," "intellectual disability," "cognitive delay," and "developmental disability" can refer to the same medical terms. "Learning disability" is used to refer to impairments, such as dyslexia, in which a person may have a high IQ but not the ability to perform certain tasks, such as reading or math. Sources for further reading about terminology are available at Peter Wright and Pamela Wright, *Wrightslaw: From Emotions to Advocacy*, 2nd ed. (Hartsfield, VA: Harbor House Law Press, 2006), 351–60 (also available at http://www.wrightslaw.com/links/glossary.sped.legal.htm); Center for Inclusive Child Care, "Special Education Terminology Glossary," http://www.inclusivechildcare.org/inclusion_glossary.cfm; and Joy J. Rogers, "Glossary of Special Education Terms," Council for Disability Rights, http://www.disabilityrights.org/glossary.htm.

38. Americans with Disabilities Act of 1990, Public Law 101-336, 101st Cong., 2nd sess. (July 26, 1990), 104 Stat. 327.

39. Department of Justice, Disability Rights Section, "Maintaining Accessibility in Museums," http://www.ada.gov/business/museum_access.htm (accessed November 29, 2012).

40. Department of Justice, Disability Rights Section, "Maintaining Accessibility in Museums."

41. Association of Science-Technology Centers, "Resource Center: Accessible Practices: Museums' Legal Obligations," http://www.astc.org/resource/access/obligations.htm (accessed January 10, 2013).

42. Department of Justice, "ADA Requirements for Small Towns," March 2000, http://www.ada.gov/smtown.htm#anchor15334 (accessed January 13, 2013).

43. Vicky Woollard, "Caring for the Visitor," in International Council of Museums, *Running a Museum*, 105.

44. United Nations, "United Nations Universal Declaration of Human Rights 1948," http://www.un.org/en/documents/udhr/index.shtml (accessed January 27, 2013)

45. Woollard, "Caring for the Visitor," 107.

Chapter Two

Sensitivity and Awareness

Preparing the Museum Staff

From 2009 to 2010, the percentage of the total U.S. population with a disability grew by 2.0 percentage points, according to a study from the American Association of People with Disabilities. The study counted 304,287,836 people living in the United States, 36,354,712 of them having some kind of disability.[1] Many of these individuals attend public schools, are part of the workforce, live independently, and are increasingly visible members of every community. Many are elderly, a group that has long been a healthy slice of the museumgoing audience. Thirty-six million Americans with disabilities offer a challenge and opportunity for educational professionals at museums and historic sites.

As museums and historic sites become transformed into community centers and open spaces for all people, the first step to take when welcoming people with disabilities is awareness and sensitivity to people. In many instances, teachers and individuals have chosen not to visit a museum or historic site, as they may not have felt welcome because of the fragility of artifacts or structures or physical barriers or may have felt uneasy about disturbing other visitors or staff. Museums can seem intimidating. When museums make changes that increase access for those with disabilities, it can mean more visitors; in other words, enabling one person with a disability to visit often brings at least two people to the museum.

At the 2012 Tennessee Association of Museums conference in Memphis, Tennessee, I chaired a panel titled "Your Museum: Compliance, Awareness, Sensitivity, and Outreach." The panelists intended their session to reach professionals at small museums and to give them the tools necessary to engage visitors with disabilities. The session explored ways in which museum professionals have adapted their sites and exhibits to comply with the Americans with Disabilities Act (ADA). The panelists offered sensitivity and awareness techniques as well as options for professionals at small and/or low-budget museums to assist people with disabilities. The session also offered ideas about community stewardship and ways that regional museums can reach and involve local nonprofits that serve populations with disabilities.

The session's origin stemmed from a discussion with colleagues about the spring 2005 special issue of the *Public Historian*, which addressed disability and museums.[2] The articles range in subject matter from Franklin Delano Roosevelt to the experiences of visitors who are visually impaired at a museum to reviews of websites and books. Striking in this selection of readings were the firsthand accounts of people with disabilities and their experiences at museums. Their stories spoke of a lack of compassion, sensitivity, and even awareness. Their stories of limited experiences led to discussions about what museums can do to welcome more people.

As museum professionals research ways to include people with disabilities, the limited museum literature about the inclusion of those who have intellectual disabilities is apparent. Since the implementation of ADA, so much of the focus has been on wheelchair accessibility and assistance for the sight and hearing impaired, but in many cases, those with learning disabilities are forgotten. In the real world of limited resources and personnel at most of the nation's museums, finding the time and the funding to conduct training is nearly impossible. I hoped that the session would give some ideas, discussion, and thinking points for staff members at small museums.[3]

SENSITIVITY AND AWARENESS: STRATEGIES AND TECHNIQUES FOR WELCOMING ALL VISITORS

In general, people with disabilities are like everyone else and desire to be treated the same as any visitor at a museum or historic site. An important definition that people should remember is this: "A disability is a condition that limits a person's ability to walk, talk, see, hear, or reason. A handicap is an imposed barrier that restricts a person. People with disabilities are handicapped by society's mistaken beliefs about their disabilities."[4] Professionals in museums should consider disabilities as challenges, not burdens.

To begin to welcome people with disabilities at your historic site or museum, it is important to first recognize that each visitor is a person who deserves respect. Often, people with disabilities are viewed as victims or threats or are seen as someone to pity or view as a hero. Some people view those with disabilities as unable to participate or unworthy of being recognized. With more complete information, such misunderstandings can be avoided.

It is important to remember that there are both visible and invisible disabilities. Visible disabilities include people who use mobility aids, such as crutches or wheelchairs, physical differences, or motor impairments. Invisible disabilities are myriad and can include people with hearing or vision difficulties, learning disabilities, or cognitive disabilities.

The first goal is to create a more welcoming environment and to provide an atmosphere of acceptance. Language is a first step. One should always remember to put the person before the disability. For example, the phrase "the person with low vision" should be used in place of "the blind person." This person-first language shows respect by putting the person before the disability. Additionally, one should always emphasize abilities rather than point out what a person cannot do. Another suggestion is to always avoid labels and never refer to a person by his or her disability. For example, do not say "the handicapped, the crippled, the blind." The presentation emphasized that people often use negative language without realizing it; a conscious effort to humanize the person rather than focusing on the disability will help curb this practice. Professionals should always listen to themselves and make changes as necessary when interacting with people with disabilities.

Another basic is body language since it offers important clues about what you are saying. When interacting with people with low vision or hearing difficulty in particular, one should always face the person and keep his or her face in full light. Just as important is attitude. A patronizing attitude, such as patting people who use wheelchairs on the head, never helps. While one hopes that such behavior is not something that happens on a regular basis, it does. Additionally, one should not lean or hang on someone's wheelchair; people should always remember that people with physical disabilities treat their wheelchairs as extensions of their bodies.

Guide dogs and other service animals are common among people with disabilities, and there are several guidelines for interacting with animals and their people. Service animals are very busy working, and their attention is on several things at one time. Since the animals are working, it is never acceptable to distract, pet, or bother an animal while it is working.

An often overlooked aspect of accessibility for museums is website development. The ADA website offers strategies for ensuring that websites are accessible to those with visual and other impairments.[5] Because many people with disabilities use technology on computers and the Internet, it is important to make sure the website is accessible for screen readers and voice recognition software. The ADA website recommends using "screen-reader-accessible web design, adjustable font and color contrast, and high-contrast images."[6] Additionally, the ADA provides guidelines for web developers, including a checklist from the Web Accessibility Initiative.[7]

It is also important to remember to include people with disabilities in the planning and development stages of programs, exhibits, and events. Creating focus groups, working with people in the community, and reaching out to classes and senior citizen groups will make the museum's job easier while including the community they hope to attract.

One of the best examples of integration and inclusion among professionals in the United States is the Museum Access Consortium (MAC) in New York City. The MAC consists of representatives from various museum departments throughout the metropolitan area and members and representatives of the disability community. Members of MAC exchange information, ideas, and resources and provide a network of mutual support. The MAC includes among its members persons with personal and professional experience with disabilities and accessibility.[8]

The British Museum in London published a "Disability Etiquette Scheme" on its website.[9] The document outlines the museum's philosophy on accessibility and etiquette for staff and visitors and summarizes the current and future opportunities that the museum offers for people with disabilities. To ensure that it complies with legal obligations and good practices, the museum consults individuals with disabilities and various organizations.[10] In addition to meetings, the museum uses face-to-face consultation, partnerships with local and national disability groups, telephone and e-mail consultation, focus groups, and visitor feedback.[11]

All museums should create partnerships and consultation groups that include community members who have disabilities. Professionals can contact their local government, organizations dedicated to specific and various disabilities, and individuals in the community to form these valuable groups.

WORKSHOPS AND TRAINING OPPORTUNITIES

I organized a workshop in 2012 at Middle Tennessee State University titled "Disability and Your Cultural Organization: Sensitivity and Strategies for Going beyond ADA" in an effort to raise awareness among regional museum professionals. The forum included professionals from across the United States to address disability topics as they relate to museums and other historical organizations and sites. The workshop served as a symposium to provide resources and support to public organizations to develop and improve program offerings to the underserved community of students and adults with disabilities. The program also provided an opportunity for professionals to learn best practices to help small museums with limited resources to be more inclusive in their programs and exhibits.

Fifteen professionals from Tennessee museums, historic sites, and universities from Memphis to Sevierville attended the workshop. The speakers at this event included keynote speaker Krista Flores from the Smithsonian Institution Accessibility Program, who addressed the major issues of accessibility in museums; Karen Wade, director of the Homestead Museum in Los Angeles County, California, who shared her experiences with welcoming diverse audiences; and Dr. Lisa Pruitt of the Middle Tennessee State University history department, who spoke about disability history in the context of the workshop.

A panel discussion followed the speakers, and it proved to be a lively discussion about museums and accessibility. The panel consisted of Dr. Bill Norwood from the Tennessee Rehabilitation Center; Andi Halbert, who is a recreational therapist; and Dr. Brenden Martin from the Middle Tennessee State University history department. Following lunch, participants joined four work sessions to discuss specific ideas and challenges on the topics of museum and exhibit design, sensory impairments, strategies for the physically impaired, and cognitive and developmental delay.

Krista Flores works in an office with three other accessibility associates, and their main tasks include increasing tactile components of exhibits and programs, increasing universal design, and working with various disabilities individually to create programs that are more effective. For instance, through the efforts of the accessibility program, the Smithsonian family of museums now offers tours with a docent who offers basic verbal description and label reading for those with visual impairments. Flores also emphasized integrating people with disabilities into programs so that they can experience the museum as anyone else would.

Flores indicated three key components for creating accessible spaces: effective communication, readily achievable barrier removal, and integration. Effective communication is essential in conveying the main themes of any exhibit to people with disabilities. Barrier removal for exhibits is also essential for mobility throughout the exhibit space or museum. Flores suggested doing what is possible in the best way that the museum is capable, but she also recognized that sometimes this is not possible with historic structures or large museum spaces. Integration of people with disabilities into the displays and as visitors is also important, as is the ability to make choices; as with any other visitor, those with disabilities may want to skip a gallery or exhibit, so this should be an option when designing accessible features or programs. The next chapter focuses on barrier-free learning and universal design options for museums.

Karen Wade presented a case study from the Homestead Museum in California. Wade focused on the future of museums and disability as well the aging population in the United States. According to Wade, by 2030, 20 percent of the U.S. population will be over the age of sixty-five, which presents many challenges for museums to create an atmosphere that is welcoming to that demographic. The Homestead Museum has implemented integration and universal design elements, but some of its biggest success has come from specialized programs for senior citizens. Specialized programs could be beneficial for all disabilities; while integration and universal design are wonderful, specialized programs for various populations can be accommodating if resources are available to create those programs.

The panel discussion and presentation gave participants the chance to ask questions and discuss various techniques available for historic sites and museums. Bill Norwood, Brenden Martin, and Andi Halbert facilitated the discussion (see figure 2.1). Halbert discussed what recreation therapy is and how it can be utilized at various sites. Martin supported a conversation about challenges that museums face; participants opened up in this discussion about the challenges and barriers at their respective sites. Norwood, who specializes in work services for people with disabilities, also offered museums the chance to employ people with disabilities at their site as docents or volunteers.

Of the fifteen individuals at the event, eleven took a survey immediately after the event, and five of those participants completed a follow-up survey in February 2013. The survey results indicated that participants did become more aware of etiquette and sensitivity. Answers to the question "What did you learn that you plan to implement in your job/life?" from the survey immediately following the workshop included "Just to be more cognizant of universal design; also, implement etiquette training" and "The whole attitude that the disability comes from people and buildings that do not properly accommodate impaired people."

In the follow-up survey in February 2013, three answers indicated that the participants had used ideas of techniques presented at the workshop in their professional life, while two were unsure. Those individuals who did use something from the workshop in their professional lives said that they had

Figure 2.1.   Bill Norwood, Brenden Martin, and Andi Halbert in panel discussion

used it in drafting interpretation plans and in academic research. One museum put the techniques discussed at the workshop to practical use. The participant explained that

> because of spatial, lighting and sound changes throughout our building, ceiling and flooring variations, and frequent encounters with the 42-foot statue, 24-foot doors and enormous columns, any awareness and advance preparation for these adjustments can help to alleviate stress and create a more enjoyable museum experience. We had not thought of offering this service before attending the workshop. [12]

Another response indicated that the museum is working to develop a video tour, photo book, and tactile objects for anyone who visits the site displaying the use of universal design and barrier-free exhibits that were discussed in the workshop. Such results were the intended result of the workshop, and it is very rewarding to know that, even if they are small or incremental, changes are being made in the region to accommodate people with disabilities.

Overall, such comments as "it was a valuable and meaningful workshop, and I intend to keep disability access issues in mind as a public history professional," "thank you very much for offering the workshop. It was amazing," and "it was a great workshop, and I'm so glad that I attended" indicate that those who did attend the workshop believed that it was a valuable use of their time and resources.

There are many organizations that offer disability awareness, sensitivity, and etiquette training opportunities. The Museum of Disability offers an on-site disability etiquette program that provides an understanding of awareness, information about misconceptions regarding disabilities, and tips for interacting with people with disabilities. [13] The Disability Etiquette Training Company is another organization that offers classes that raise awareness about disabilities. The sessions are available through teleconference, on the Internet, or in person. [14]

The British Museum's "Disability Awareness Scheme" also includes information about staff training. The pamphlet details information about the staff training programs and states, "The Museum recognises its responsibility for the actions of its employees during the course of their employment." [15] The British Museum offers training for all museum employees and volunteers through the SHAPE program, training for all visitor service and security staff by the access manager employed by the museum, and visual awareness training for visitor service staff.

The Museum of London offers volunteer training on disability etiquette. The guidelines for the program are available on the Museum of London website, and they can easily be adapted for other museums to use for staff training. [16] The three-hour workshop offers participants the opportunity to understand the diversity of people with disabilities, to learn ways they can make the museum and activities at the museum more accessible to people with disabilities, and to gain confidence and competence in communications. The Disability Action Group in Islington, England, originally designed the course.[17]

From the front-desk staff to security guards and janitorial staff, all museum employees need to have some sort of training to understand how to interact with diverse visitors. All staff should know general basics of working with and assisting people with disabilities. Training opportunities are myriad, and more tips are offered in the following chapters of this manual.

MUSEUMS LEADING BY EXAMPLE

Several museums in the United States have developed innovative programs and opportunities for both staff and the public to learn more about disabilities and sensitivity. Many times, art and children's museums are the leaders in accessibility awareness and programming. Following is a sampling of several model programs from all types of museums.

The Boston Children's Museum for the Youth Museum Exhibit Collaborative created a disability awareness exhibit called *Access/ABILITY*, which has been featured at several museums, including San Diego's Museum of Man, the Philadelphia Please Touch Museum, and the George Bush Presidential Library and Museum at Texas A&M University.[18] The website describes the exhibit as, "highly interactive . . . delivers the message to children, parents and educators that as human beings, we are more alike than different."[19] The exhibit includes activities that demonstrate that all people have similarities and differences regardless of ability level. Interactive audience participation includes learning American Sign Language, writing using Braille, and a multisensory City Walk.[20]

In 2009, the Please Touch Museum in Philadelphia hosted an Autism Awareness Night. For one evening, the museum was open to families and children with autism. A blog posted on the museum's website contained the testimony of a mother, Monica, who took her family to the event. This mother described the trepidation she felt when visiting museums: "Some of our concerns were the crowds and how other kids would interact with Jesse since he does not speak, but uses a talking device. Worse yet, the stares from staff members we have experienced during visits to other locations."[21] She went on to describe the educational and welcoming environment that the family was exposed to at the museum. Monica closed by saying, "As a special needs parent, nights like this are often hard to come by. I so appreciate all that Please Touch Museum does for families of children with special needs."[22]

The following year, in 2010, the Please Touch Museum opened for a Disability Awareness Night for all children and families with disabilities. The event included hands-on and sensory activities, and the light levels and loud noises were changed to make the experience more comfortable for people with sensory disabilities. In addition to creating a special environment for children with disabilities, the museum hosted several local resource organizations for family members and caregivers.[23]

The Intrepid Sea, Air & Space Museum Complex introduced its Disability Awareness Month in October 2012. The event included family activities, tours, and speaking events. Their website stated that the goal of this month-long event was

> to bring together families, children, and adults with varying special needs, and advocates who are involved with creating and supporting opportunities for them. From children to adults who are, or work with, the deaf or hard-of-hearing, blind or partially-sighted, or are affected by autism, this month celebrates our differences and raises awareness for bettering cultural experiences for everyone.[24]

By including all disabilities and age-groups, this program was designed to incorporate all people and create a welcoming environment for them at the museum.

Finally, the art initiative Art Beyond Sight has a website dedicated to information about using art at museums to reach audiences with sight impairment.[25] The website offers many suggestions and ideas that all museums, not just art museums, can adapt for use at their own sites. It suggests reaching out to museum employees to talk about sensitivity and awareness, training security guards and front-desk staff on awareness and sensitivity techniques, talking with community members, inviting an artist or a speaker who has a visual impairment, and creating partnerships with schools. These are great suggestions for any museum, not just those that work solely with visual arts.

Historic sites and small museums can create more welcoming and diverse programs by adapting any of these exhibits or programming ideas. Communities can be made more welcoming and involved in the formation of these events. Involving those with disabilities in the development and planning stages is crucial to success.

NOTES

1. American Association of People with Disabilities and the Employment Practices and Measurement Rehabilitation Research Training Center at the University of New Hampshire, *2011 Annual Disability Statistics Compendium* (Durham: University of New Hampshire Institute on Disability, 2011).

2. Susan Burch and Katherine Ott, eds., "Disability and the Practice of Public History," special issue, *Public Historian* 27 (Spring 2005).

3. I originally compiled this information for the presentation "Sensitivity and Awareness: Steps to Take for Successful Connections" at the Tennessee Association of Museums Conference, March 2012. Information from several sources was used, including Judith Cohen, "Etiquette," Community Resources for Independence, http://www.crinet.org/education/independent%20Living/etiquette (accessed April 4, 2012); Disability Resource Agency for Independent Living, "Disability Awareness Sensitivity Training Presentation," http://www.cflic.org/disability%20Awareness%20Sensitivity%20 (accessed April 4, 2012); and Tennessee Disability Coalition, "Disability Etiquette: Engaging People with Disabilities," http://www.tndisability.org/system/files/ul/Disability_Etiquette.pdf (accessed April 4, 2012).

4. Disability Resource Agency for Independent Living, "Disability Awareness Sensitivity Training Presentation."

5. U.S. Department of Justice, "Maintaining Accessibility at Museums," http://www.ada.gov/business/museum_access.htm (accessed April 5, 2013).

6. U.S. Department of Justice, "Accessibility of State and Local Government Websites to People with Disabilities," http://www.ada.gov/websites2.htm (accessed April 6, 2013).

7. Web Accessibility Initiative, "Web Content Accessibility Guidelines," http://www.w3c.org/WAI/Resources (accessed September 1, 2013).

8. Museum Access Consortium, "What Is the Museum Access Consortium (MAC)?" http://www.cityaccessny.org/mac.php (accessed April 4, 2013).

9. British Museum, "Disability Etiquette Scheme," http://www.britishmuseum.org/pdf/disability.pdf (accessed August 28, 2013).

10. British Museum, "Disability Etiquette Scheme."

11. British Museum, "Disability Etiquette Scheme."

12. From the results of the February 2013 workshop survey, in the author's possession.

13. Museum of Disability, "Disability Etiquette Programs," http://museumofdisability.org/visitor-information/activities/disability-etiquette-programs (accessed August 21, 2013).

14. Disability Etiquette Training Company, "Home Page," http://www.disabilityetiquettetraining.com (accessed August 22, 2013).

15. Disability Etiquette Training Company, "Home Page."

16. Museum of London, "Disability Equality Training for Volunteers," http://www.museumoflondon.org.uk/.../DisabilityAwareness_TrainingPlan.doc (accessed August 27, 2013).

17. Museum of London, "Disability Equality Training for Volunteers."

18. Youth Museum Exhibit Collaborative, "Access/ABILITY," http://www.ymec.org/ex_access.html (accessed August 15, 2013).

19. Youth Museum Exhibit Collaborative, "Access/ABILITY."

20. Youth Museum Exhibit Collaborative, "Access/ABILITY."

21. Pinky's Please Touch Museum, "Meet My New Friends!" http://pleasetouchmuseum.blogspot.com/2010/04/meet-my-new-friends.html (accessed August 16, 2013).

22. Pinky's Please Touch Museum, "Meet My New Friends!"

23. Pinky's Please Touch Museum, "PTM & Variety's Disability Awareness Night," http://pleasetouchmuseum.blogspot.com/2010/08/ptm-varietys-disability-awareness-night.html (accessed August 16, 2013).

24. Intrepid Sea, Air & Space Museum Complex, "Disability Awareness Month," http://www.intrepidmuseum.org/DisabilityAwarenessMonth.aspx (accessed August 17, 2013).

25. Art Beyond Sight, "How to Celebrate at Museums," http://www.artbeyondsight.org/change/aw-c-museums.shtml (accessed August 18, 2013).

Chapter Three

Universal Design at Museums and Historic Sites

Once museum and historic site staff members learn sensitivity and awareness techniques to work with people with disabilities, the staff must continue along the road to accessibility and full inclusion by following universal design techniques in exhibits, physical spaces, and program offerings. The Americans with Disabilities Act (ADA) requires museums and historic sites to comply with accessibility standards to the maximum level possible, but the ADA typically defines "accessibility" as physical convenience to those with mobility, hearing, or sight impairments. Universal design creates spaces and experiences that provide the maximum accessibility for *all* people, all the time, regardless of ability, age, impairment, or knowledge.

Universal design, originally an architectural concept, encompasses everything from signage and way-finding materials to written text and lighting to access to space and objects within structures. The importance of universal design is apparent by the number of people with disabilities in the United States. The American Association of People with Disabilities counted 36,354,712 people in the United States in 2010 living with a disability. As that number increases by as much as 2 percent per year, the need for accessible opportunities becomes more imperative. Sites that implement universal design maintain accessibility without barriers to any visitor.

With an increased aging population due to the baby-boomer population, disabilities became more prominent throughout the United States beginning in the 1970s. Legislation for people with disabilities in the 1970s, 1980s, and 1990s, such as the Rehabilitation Act of 1973, the Individuals with Disabilities Education Act, and the ADA, sparked the movement for universal use in the structural design of buildings. As architects began to design with ADA compliance in mind, the results were often distracting and not aesthetically pleasing. The idea of universal design was born from this realization and a dedication to improve accessibility by creating spaces usable by all audiences without visibly overt accessibility design.

The Center for Universal Design at the North Carolina State University College of Design is a research, information, and assistance center that evaluates and develops accessible and universal design. [1] The center explains that universal design "is the design of products and environments to be usable by all people" and that it exists to simplify life for all individuals regardless of age or ability. [2] The center also publicized its seven principles of universal design in 1997. The principles are (1) equitable use, (2) flexibility in use, (3) simple and intuitive use, (4) perceptible information, (5) tolerance for error, (6) low physical effort, and (7) size and space for approach and use. [3] This chapter explores these principles and real-world examples, and the following chapter describes model educational programs for people with disabilities at museums across the United States.

According to Universal Designers and Consultants, Inc., "Universal Design involves designing products and spaces so that they can be used by the widest range of people possible. Universal Design evolved from Accessible Design, a design process that addresses the needs of people with disabilities." [4] Universal design not only benefits those individuals with disabilities who utilize the space but also helps all people have a more positive experience. For example, a sidewalk (figure 3.1) with a wheelchair ramp from the street benefits not only individuals who have mobility problems but also those using strollers, bicycles, and other wheeled vehicles. As the Universal Designers and Consultants, Inc., group explained, "By designing for this human diversity, we can create things that will be easier for all people to use." [5]

A design book published in 2010 presented universal design elements of all types for artists and architects. The book, *Universal Principles of Design*, explains that buildings, spaces, objects, and signage "should be usable by people of diverse abilities, without special adaptation or modification." [6] The authors presented four characteristics of accessibility in universal design: perceptibility, operability, simplicity, and forgiveness. Perceptibility provides the opportunity for all people to perceive the design, even if they cannot see or otherwise sense it. Operability, which means that everyone can use the design in question regardless of his or her physical abilities, is the second characteristic of accessibility. Designers who use simplicity ensure that anyone, regardless of experience, literacy, or concentration level, has an equitable experience. Forgiveness in design minimizes the occurrence of errors in the design or in human interaction with the design. Universal design uses many different methods to achieve encompassing sensory elements, and museums and historic sites can learn from those experiences to provide exhibits that are more interesting for all visitors.

Museums and historic sites can also benefit from universal design practices to meet the ADA's requirements for accessibility and to better serve and attract visitors. For museums specifically, Janice Majewski from the Smithsonian Institution Accessibility Program authored guidelines for creating accessible and barrier-free universally designed exhibits that are available online through the Smithsonian Institution's website.[7] Majewski emphasizes that universal design is not a trend, but it "must be a part of this new philosophy of exhibition development because people with disabilities are a part of museums' diverse audience."[8] This is an evolving field, and design tools offered in the document are not fixed solutions; each museum or historic home must mix, match, and test the suggested solutions to find what works best for a specific organization.[9] It is important to remember that no one fix will work for every museum. The guidelines do offer suggestions and examples for exhibit content and items as well as accessible label design, lighting, and spaces, all of which are helpful to any historic site or museum.

Small museums and historic sites still deal with a learning curve of design and accessibility, and recognition of universal design as an important aspect of museum programming is the first step toward successful universal design programming. In 2002, Steve Tokar surveyed 158 science museums on their understanding and use of universal design techniques.[10] One question asked if the person who filled out the survey was familiar with the term "universal design." In museums with fewer than 100,000 visitors per year, 47 percent of respondents were familiar with the term, but in museums with more than 1 million visitors per year, 73 percent of respondents were familiar with the term. Smaller museums often have a small staff and limited budget, decreasing the opportunities for professional development and conference attendance. E-mail listservs and other communication with staff members across the world have increased awareness about trends and success stories at museums, but a financial and opportunity gap frequently remains between large and small museums.

Interestingly, according to Tokar's survey, the number of universally designed exhibits in both demographics was 67 percent. Identified challenges of universal design included cost (43 percent), "can't be all things for all people" (30 percent), and space (19 percent).[11] In those museums that did offer universal design, examples given were wheelchair access, hands-on/multisensory exhibits, and general accessibility.[12] Tokar concluded that the wide range of examples shows that "universal design" means something different to each museum professional or museum. For some, it is accessibility for individuals with disabilities, but for others, it means design for all visitors regardless of ability.[13] Because large-budget science and children museums often lead the way for the rest of the museum world, universal design became better recognized among professionals through conferences, workshops, and communications with other staff members.

There are unique challenges to create universally designed accessible spaces in preexisting historic structures and museum buildings. The ADA.gov website offers suggestions and helpful tips for creating universally designed and accessible buildings without destroying the historical integrity of structures. Many museum professionals are using creative fixes to construct spaces that are more accessible.

Museums generally face problems with entrances and mobility within structures, but universal design techniques create environments that are both accessible for those individuals with mobility issues and useful to all members of the museum audience. According to the ADA, accessible routes that provide entrance and egress from the building must be marked, clear, and open at all times. The doors should also be power operated to open and close, though if that is not available, staff should be there at all times to open and close doors for people who cannot. [14] As visitors enter the building, all want to experience the museum in the same way regardless of ability. All audiences should benefit from the design of exhibits, events, brochures, videos, and programs. The following chapter provides more information and tips for creating educational programming that reaches a wide audience.

Historic buildings provide more challenges and opportunities for universal design, yet they provide opportunities for innovation in creating accessible and universally designed spaces. The ADA requires that historic buildings be accessible and compliant; however, there are exceptions and alternatives provided in the "frequently asked questions" section of the ADA's website. [15] Historic properties must comply with ADA accessibility guidelines for historic properties "to the highest extent feasible." [16] If these provisions will destroy the historic features of the building, an advisory board can offer consultation to provide alternatives. For example, historic buildings may use ramps that are steeper than is usually permitted to save space, and accessible routes are required on the level of the accessible entrance. In the rare case that the building's structural and historical integrity prevents accessibility, the staff can develop programs that provide alternative information to visitors who cannot physically enter the building. [17] Universal design in historic structures remains a complicated subject; creative museum staffs continue to create programming options and complementary substitutions to create equitable experiences for all visitors.

MUSEUMS UTILIZING UNIVERSAL DESIGN SUCCESSFULLY

As is usually the case, museums with a focus on science and art have some of the best programs and resources to create accessible programs. The Boston Museum of Science, the Metropolitan Museum of Art, and the Royal Ontario Museum created exhibition spaces for the enjoyment of all audiences.

Figure 3.1. Universal design example

The Boston Museum of Science first began designing accessible exhibits over twenty-five years ago, beginning with dioramas that featured a tactile component: deer antlers were available for visitors to touch in the natural history habitat exhibits.[18] The museum added audio components as well as ingenious scent elements that provided an interactive sensory exhibit for visitors with a range of sensory abilities. More recently, the museum started incorporating programs for people with autism, learning disabilities, and cognitive disabilities. All these programs are a part of the bigger commitment to universal design and content development.

The museum's project manager for research and evaluation, Anna Lindgren-Streicher, emphasized the importance of universal design for museums:

> A commitment to a universal design approach means that the exhibit teams will work to create experiences that are accessible and educational for a broad range of visitors along the spectrum of able to disabled. Universal design also acknowledges that the design of environments and exhibits can determine whether visitors are "able" to engage in an activity and learn from it.[19]

The commitment to universal design (not only for accessibility for disabilities) is again apparent on the "accessibility" section of the museum's website, which states, "Barriers to access, whether caused by finances, culture, language, education, or ability, can inhibit exploration. The Museum is intent on breaking down these barriers while creating relationships with new audiences."[20] The web page goes on to list programs and opportunities for all visitors to enjoy and learn.

The exhibit teams at the Boston Museum of Science strive to provide for all visitors the opportunity to physically interact with the space, cognitively engage with materials, and interact socially with other visitors. The museum staff makes sure to ask questions as to the plan and design of exhibits and programs to be sure that the environment is inclusive, comfortable, and safe for diverse visitors.

To create and evaluate these programs, the museum invites volunteers with disabilities of all kinds to visit the museum and provide feedback for development. The museum continues to lead the way for all museums to become completely inclusive and barrier free; historical museums and sites can learn from and adapt their programs and ideas to meet the needs of their own audiences.

More recently, the Metropolitan Museum of Art in New York City hosted a "seeing through drawing" event. At the event, visitors with sight impairments touched sculptures and works of art, assisted by museum staff, and drew what they "saw" from that experience and from staff describing objects to them.[21] The museum also provided American Sign Language tours for visitors with hearing impairments. All of this is part of a bigger program that invites any visitor, including those with a range of disabilities, to visit the museum for a multisensory experience. The program includes scent, touch, music and verbal imaging, and description. Although the museum initially designed the program for people with disabilities, the multisensory engagement can be a new experience for all visitors.

In 2010, the Royal Ontario Museum (ROM) in Toronto, Ontario, opened the "most accessible exhibition in the ROM's history."[22] The exhibit, *The Warrior Emperor and China's Terracotta Army*, included reproductions of exhibits on display that visitors could touch and feel. In addition, the museum provided Braille and large-print booklets for visitors with sight impairment. For visitors with hearing impairments, the museum offered captioned video materials and transcripts of podcasts related to the exhibit on their website. The exhibit resides in a hall of the museum that is accessible by elevator, and the length of the exhibit hall provided more seating than had previously been available in exhibits. The extra seating provides a place of rest for all visitors, even those without disabilities.

In the press release published on the museum's website, the head of visitor experience, Cheryl Blackman, stated, "The ROM is committed, through its Accessibility Strategy to remove barriers to participation for its visitors with disabilities."[23] Although this is not universal design by name but rather accessibility design, the product creates a welcoming and comfortable environment for any visitor. Additionally, the strategy cites elevator and way-finding materials as accessible offerings of the museum. The ROM's accessibility strategy provides audio guides, tactile displays, and digital access to collections, benefiting any visitor.[24]

More recently, in 2012, the ROM opened *Maya: Secrets of their Ancient World*, which included fourteen touchable reproductions of sculptures, masks, and ceramics featured in the display.[25] This addition confirms the dedication of the museum to create multisensory accessible exhibits and programs for their visitors that conform to universal design principles. All visitors, from children to adults, with a wide variety of abilities, experience learning more effectively when tactile and multisensory implements are used. These universal design techniques enhance the overall educational experience for all visitors.

All these examples are from large institutions with a wide variety of visitors and large budgets. Small museums and historic sites often do not have the monetary or spatial resources to implement such large-scale programs. However, the following chapters explore ways that other museums adopt universal design and specialized programs.

UNIVERSAL DESIGN IN LEARNING

Schools across the United States implement universal design into teacher training and curriculum. Educators recognize that universal design for learning is beneficial for all students, not just those in special education classes. *Universal Design for Learning: A Guide for Teachers and Education Professionals*, published by the Council for Exceptional Children (CEC), explains universal design techniques to teachers and offers examples of application in the classroom. Museums can also use the information from this book to provide universally designed compliant educational programs.[26] The CEC explains, "Universal design provides equal access to learning, not simply equal access to information. Universal design allows the student to control the method of accessing information while the teacher monitors the learning process and initiates any beneficial methods. . . . Universal design promotes effective teaching."[27] This method puts learning in the hands of the students, with the teacher or museum staff as the facilitator and assistant.

The guide also provides Four Essential Features of Universal Design in Learning. The four essentials ensure that the lesson (1) represents information in multiple formats and media, (2) provides multiple pathways for students' actions and expressions, (3) provides multiple ways to engage students' interests and motivation, and (4) occurs in a safe environment.[28]

The nature of learning, according to the CEC, is an active and individual process that must occur in an engaging and safe environment.[29] Museum educators should remember these aspects as they create lesson plans and programs for any group. Active experiences shape and provide a memorable learning experience, and engaging programs involve attention directly as well as peripheral perception. The whole individual is the target audience for programs so that each person can experience the lesson from his or her own vantage point. Providing this experience in a nonjudgmental and physically safe environment ensures full attention to the learning experience.[30]

Rather than providing exclusive programs for people with disabilities, museums should strive to create a wholly inclusive environment for all visitors to have the same experience to the highest degree possible. However, there are times when specific programs can be adapted for visitors with specials needs of any kind. Universal design may be a utopian and unrealistic goal for many small museums and historic sites because of architectural features, limited budgets, and small staff. Sites need to realize that no matter how hard they try, they cannot always be all things to everyone.

Working with teachers, students, and focus groups, museums can create successful specialized programs to meet the needs of specific groups of people with disabilities. The following chapters outline specific programs for people with autism, dementia, mobility impairments, or other disabilities.

NOTES

1. Center for Universal Design, "About the Center," http://www.ncsu.edu/ncsu/design/cud/about_us/about_us.htm (accessed October 4, 2013).

2. Center for Universal Design, "About Universal Design," http://www.ncsu.edu/ncsu/design/cud/about_ud/about_ud.htm (accessed October 4, 2013).

3. Center for Universal Design, *The Principles of Universal Design*, ver. 2.0 (Raleigh: North Carolina State University, 1997). Full list available at http://www.ncsu.edu/ncsu/design/cud/about_ud/udprinciplestext.htm (accessed October 18, 2013).

4. Universal Designers and Consultants, Inc., "What Is Universal Design?" http://www.universaldesign.com/about-universal-design.html (accessed October 5, 2013).

5. Universal Designers and Consultants, Inc., "What Is Universal Design?"

6. William Lidwell, Kritina Holden, and Jill Butler, *Universal Principles of Design* (Beverly, MA: Rockport Publishers, 2010).

7. Janice Majewski, "Smithsonian Guidelines for Accessible Exhibition Design," Smithsonian Accessibility Program, http://accessible.si.edu/pdf/Smithsonian%20Guidelines%20for%20accessible%20design.pdf (accessed October 17, 2013).

8. Majewski, "Smithsonian Guidelines for Accessible Exhibition Design."

9. Majewski, "Smithsonian Guidelines for Accessible Exhibition Design," ii.

10. Steve Tokar, "Universal Design in North American Museums with Hands-On Science Exhibits: A Survey," *Visitor Studies Today* 7, issue 3 (Fall/Winter 2004): 6–10.

11. Tokar, "Universal Design in North American Museums with Hands-On Science Exhibits," 9.

12. Tokar, "Universal Design in North American Museums with Hands-On Science Exhibits," 10.

13. Tokar, "Universal Design in North American Museums with Hands-On Science Exhibits," 10.

14. Americans with Disabilities Act, "Maintaining Accessibility in Museums," http://www.ada.gov/business/museum_access.htm (accessed September 17, 2013).

15. Americans with Disabilities Act, "ADA Frequently Asked Questions," http://www.ada.gov/pubs/t2qa.txt (accessed September 17, 2013).

16. Americans with Disabilities Act, "ADA Frequently Asked Questions."

17. Americans with Disabilities Act, "ADA Frequently Asked Questions."

18. "Boston Museum of Science Incorporates Unique Accessibility Experiment," *The Examiner*, August 20, 2012, http://www.examiner.com/article/boston-museum-of-science-incorporates-unique-accessibility-experiment (accessed October 12, 2013).

19. "Boston Museum of Science Incorporates Unique Accessibility Experiment."

20. Boston Museum of Science, "Accessibility," http://www.mos.org/accessibility#a-place-for-everyone (accessed October 12, 2013).

21. Tanya Mohn, "Welcoming Art Lovers with Disabilities," *New York Times*, October 25, 2013.

22. Royal Ontario Museum, "The Warrior Emperor Is the Most Accessible Exhibition in the ROM's History," August 24, 2010, http://www.rom.on.ca/en/about-us/newsroom/press-releases/the-warrior-emperor-is-the-most-accessible-exhibition-in-the-roms (accessed October 12, 2013).

23. Royal Ontario Museum, "The Warrior Emperor Is the Most Accessible Exhibition in the ROM's History."

24. Royal Ontario Museum, "The Warrior Emperor Is the Most Accessible Exhibition in the ROM's History."

25. Jeff Hayward, "Royal Ontario Museum Focuses on Accessibility with Tactile Exhibit Design," *Design Edge Canada*, March 16, 2012.

26. Council for Exceptional Children, *Universal Design for Learning: A Guide for Teachers and Education Professionals* (Arlington, VA: Council for Exceptional Children, 2007).

27. Council for Exceptional Children, *Universal Design for Learning*, 3.

28. Council for Exceptional Children, *Universal Design for Learning*, 4.

29. Council for Exceptional Children, *Universal Design for Learning*, 32.

30. Council for Exceptional Children, *Universal Design for Learning*, 33.

Chapter Four

Model Programs of Accessibility at Museums in the United States

Multiple museums in the United States are working to better serve people with disabilities. New York City, with its myriad museums and population of diverse people, is at the forefront of this movement. The Museum Access Consortium of New York City (MAC) "consists of representatives from various museum departments throughout the New York City Metropolitan area and members and representatives of the disability community." MAC's mission is "to enable people with disabilities to access cultural facilities of all types. . . . We take as a basic tenet that increasing accessibility for people with disabilities increases accessibility for everyone."[1] Institutional members meet regularly to share information and ideas and provide support. The 170 members come from cultural organizations, consultants, disability advocates, and other sites and organizations in the city. In May 2012, I met with several MAC members to talk about their experiences with access and disability.[2] The invaluable interviews and discussions contributed to the creation of a disability access model for historic sites.

The following selected museums represent art museums, science and technology museums, and historic site and history museums. The programs highlighted vary from those offered to senior adults, to children with disabilities, and to families that have a member with a disability. All examples offer the opportunity for adaptation and integration at small museums and historic sites.

MUSEUM OF MODERN ART IN NEW YORK CITY

The accessibility program that I attended at the Museum of Modern Art (MoMA) is called "Meet Me at MoMA." Through this program, attendees "look at art in the galleries with your family and friends. . . . Discuss art with specially trained MoMA educators who discuss themes, artists, and exhibitions."[3] The museum offers the event monthly to all people with dementia and their families and/or care partners. Attendees have the opportunity to look at art in the galleries and engage in discussion about the art they view. Because art is such a subjective topic that every person can interpret in his or her own way, discussions about specific works of art can stimulate the mind and provide an educational and social experience.

The gallery talk that I attended had mostly elderly people with some younger caretakers and family members. As we went through the galleries, the guide, Paula, stopped at four important pieces throughout the hour to ask questions and get responses. The four artworks were *Starry Night* by Vincent Van Gogh, *Les Demoiselles d'Avignon* by Pablo Picasso, *Bicycle Wheel* by Marcel Duchamp, and *Christina's World* by Andrew Wyeth.[4]

The first piece visited was Van Gogh's *Starry Night* (1889). The museum was closed for this program, and being in a small group, the discussions were uninhibited and illuminating. At this painting, the guide asked such questions as "What are we looking at? What are your observations?" Participants had insightful answers, such as "It looks like lights when you take your glasses off" and that looking at this painting made an individual feel that there was "nothing little about twinkle twinkle little star." Others thought that the sky seemed to overwhelm the village, that the artist used "blobs of paint," and that the painting conveyed the feeling of a cold night by using cool colors. The guide also asked, "What feelings would you say describe the work?" Answers included "Overwhelming" and "Peaceful, but the sky is exciting."[5]

Next, participants ventured into another gallery to view *Les Demoiselles d'Avignon* (1907) by Pablo Picasso (see figure 4.1). The tour leader invited participants to study the piece and make observations and comments. Most participants agreed that the painting showed lots of women but that they were not *real* women. They found the general shape, eyes, and bodies to be strange—not soft bodies but hard and square, and the eyes were crooked. When the guide asked, "Where are they?" answers included "Hell," "A scary place," and "A studio with drapes." People described this painting as "An image of despair"; "Being of women, but the women on the right side are not human"; "They are staring at us, but there is no life"; "The image is nightmarish, aggressive, and thought it was painted by a man"; and "The women are masculine." A particularly insightful participant pointed out that perhaps the women were hiding their identities behind masks and that the African-style masks are one step further toward hiding their true selves.[6]

Figure 4.1. Participants discussing *Les Demoiselles d'Avignon* by Pablo Picasso

The intriguing sculpture *Bicycle Wheel* (1951) by Marcel Duchamp was the next piece the group visited (see figure 4.2). The comments on this piece were some of the most insightful and thoughtful. Participants said that this piece presented both a challenge and a possibility. Another person claimed the piece was simply absurd: "There are no possibilities with this piece of art!" Someone else asked the question "What makes this art? Because it is in a museum?" This led to the ever-important discussion of what art is and how something can "become" art. The point was made that if this piece stood in your basement, it would be seen as trash or as something in need of repair. Another person said that this sculpture was "not enough to be art in a museum." The guide asked what it needed to become worthy of being in an art museum. The honest answer was "It just doesn't turn me on." It was then discussed that the artist intended the piece to be considered art and that anything can be art, but that does not mean everyone will like it. Another participant said that the piece represents art on a pedestal by putting a bicycle wheel on a stool. One man who said he was a painter said he felt that his art—and any art really—is not art unless someone looks at it and reacts to it.

Figure 4.2.   "Meet Me at MoMA" participants discuss *Bicycle Wheel* by Marcel Duchamp

The last piece visited was Andrew Wyeth's *Christina's World* from 1948 (see figure 4.3). This is an example of artwork that shows a person with a disability, and discussion surrounding the artwork led to this revelation. The label that accompanies the painting did not mention the aspects of disability surrounding the art, but the guide did explain that the artist's neighbor had polio and that she is likely the person depicted in the painting. Without the guide's assistance, it seems unlikely that the typical visitor would understand the significance of the painting as related to disability.

Once the circumstances surrounding the painting were revealed, the participants added their own thoughts and ideas to interpret the painting. They said that the subject of the painting is an attractive woman and graceful, but it seems that something is wrong with her. She is desperate, disabled, and yearning to walk; has no muscle tone and chafed elbows; and resides in a bleak and barren landscape. The painting is spare and realistic, while the colors reflect a grim mood. Others pointed out that, while she is struggling, her pink dress is not desolate. She has a hard life, but she is pushing and determined.[7]

Figure 4.3. Discussion of Andrew Wyeth's *Christina's World* at "Meet Me at MoMA"

One person said that the landscape in the painting looks like western Kansas, where she grew up. The group agreed that the subject seems to be seeking something; the house is her goal.[8]

Throughout the session, the gallery guide would often repeat questions, as well as the comments and answers given by participants, more loudly so everyone could hear them. She was also very patient with the audience and made sure that everyone was comfortable and understood what was going on. The participants seemed to have a great time, and they were involved in an engaging exercise that helped stimulate their cognitive powers. The question-and-answer system seemed to work well in engaging the participants, and it seems that this would be a great way to engage any audience. The inquiry-based discussion also seemed to engage the minds of the participants and give them the opportunity to view and discuss the art in a way that they may not have otherwise been able to do.

MUSEUM OF CONTEMPORARY ART
IN JACKSONVILLE, FLORIDA

The Museum of Contemporary Art in Jacksonville, Florida, offers a long-standing, very successful model program for children with autism.[9] The program is currently in its sixth year and was started after parents and museum staff collaborated to meet a tremendous need for these programs across the country. The program, "Rainbow Artists," focuses on communication and social skills as well as art, and the museum offers it strictly for children with autism.[10]

Staff and parents started "Rainbow Artists" because of the community need for this type of program. Carol Lombardo, a parent of a child with autism, wanted to create a program for children so that they could communicate through the arts. Lombardo's daughter could speak a little but could not verbally communicate very well, so they drew pictures together. The family felt that it was important to communicate in a way that all members could understand, and she could express herself through art. The museum asked Mrs. Lombardo, "If you could have any dream program for your child growing up, what would it be?" Next, they asked her to develop the program with her family's needs in mind. Lombardo described the program development process in the Southeastern Museums Conference session as an "act of love and passion for all involved."

Kelly DeSousa, an educator who worked with the program from its inception, has an art therapy degree. She worked with a school art therapist, but she learned the most from the kids. The program originally started as a Saturday program with only five kids enrolled. DeSousa also helped develop a separate program for the parents, almost as a support group for discussion. She then went to graduate school to learn about autism populations, and when she came back to the museum after school, they were serving over 200 children with autism.

Today, the program serves an average of 250 children from 8 schools. School districts recommend the students, who come to the museum for a couple of hours during the school day and then return to their regular classrooms. "Rainbow Artists" was originally offered for elementary students and now also serves middle and high school students to fill the gap for those children who are often not offered programs as much as the younger students.

Today, the program is not only for autism but for all disabilities as well. Community members and private donors fund "Rainbow Artists"; the museum staff work with teachers to schedule trips. The museum covers transportation, materials, teachers, and staff. The therapeutic objectives of the program are to improve social skills; to encourage emotional regulation and motor skills; to decrease anxiety and increase focus, self-confidence, self-esteem, and creative self-expression; to increase abstract thinking skills and imagination; and to improve visual-spatial skills. [11]

The framework for the program is as follows:

1. One visit is made to the school by museum staff for preparation. Staff tell the students what to expect for all five senses so that there are no surprises when they come to the museum. This visit also helps plan the lessons in which the students will participate at the museum.
2. Three museum visits are made—studios (classrooms), loft (hands-on learning center), and galleries.
3. The program culminates in an exhibition for Autism Awareness Month in April.

The museum staff stress that this program is not a field trip experience but rather community-based instruction. A field trip is a visit or an isolated experience that supplements the curriculum. Community-based instruction relates to goals in the school, ongoing instruction, and continuing reinforcement and can translate to the real world instead of only the classroom. Students work on skills throughout the sessions, and parents are involved ahead of time and have a follow-up afterward.

The museum staff who created the "Rainbow Artists" program suggested the following tips for planning activities for children with autism:

• Plan for multiple levels of development
• Incorporate levels of sensory involvement
• Activities build success at any level in process and or product
• Break down activities into small steps
• Provide visual cues in the setup
• Minimize distractions
• Incorporate areas for sensory downtime
• Always have a backup plan

Especially emphasized was the need to facilitate positivity; acceptance and student-initiated decision making help the student believe that he or she can succeed.

NEW YORK CITY TRANSIT MUSEUM IN BROOKLYN, NEW YORK

An effective example of a history museum that is incorporating accessibility, particularly programs for children with special needs, is the New York City Transit Museum in Brooklyn, New York. The Metro Transit Authority operates and houses the museum in an unused but formerly operable subway tunnel. The museum contains many trains from throughout the city's subway history that visitors can explore as well as exhibits related to transportation, science, energy, and history. An educator at the Transit Museum met with me to discuss the various programs the museum offers to children with special needs.[12]

The programs was initiated because of a museum goal to focus on better programming for museum audiences. Many groups of students with disabilities visited, but there was not any special programming in place. School groups visited often to study New York history and to compare the past to the present. This museum is a perfect place for the students to be immersed in history since it is a real historical site that contains historical objects and artifacts.

Older student groups at the museum often had more severe disabilities, and they were there to learn life skills, such as how to ride the subway. To welcome and assist this population, the museum began to offer classes where students could come to learn in a safe environment. Since the museum's trains and turnstiles are in a safe location and are similar to the "real" trains in the city but do not move or have masses of New Yorkers passing through, the museum setting is the perfect place for these students (figure 4.4). The

Figure 4.4.   The New York City Transit Museum subway display

life skills programs have received great reviews from parents and educators in the community.

Visitors to the independent living program have come to the museum many times per year to learn about safety and proper behavior on a train. For instance, students were taught not to stare at people; how to sit or stand, depending on the other people on the train; where to sit; how to interact with other people; and other needed skills. Staff members from all museum departments have been involved, and some have even acted as "angry New Yorker subway riders." They even have staff act as panhandlers to teach the participants how to interact with the various people they might encounter through the transit system. This museum really engages with its community not only to tell the history of the site but to also help the visitors with their needs.

The museum also offers an after-school program called "Subway Sleuths." This program meets once a week for ten weeks and is offered to students on the autism spectrum. The program helps to build social and communication skills while also teaching some history. "Subway Sleuths" teaches the history of transit, electricity, and science in addition to life skills. Through this program, students have the opportunity, in the safe subway station environment, to put their hands on history. They also learn social skills by using historical objects and situations.

The museum is not only modifying existing programs for special needs students but also creating new programming opportunities. One program uses a visual magnetic board with images. This technique can help students build on what they already know by bringing that knowledge to the forefront using images and photographs. In the train cars, students look for five things, such as lights, seats, doors, advertisements, holds, or other features. They then compare and contrast these characteristics in trains from various time periods. If they start at the newest train and work their way back in time, they will realize that, as they go back in time, there is no longer air conditioning, plastic, or other modern attributes.

In structuring tours for children with special needs, the museum educators saw that language was important. Educators use the inquiry method: "Is this train newer or older than the last train we were in?" Thinking about using language in a particular way can be overwhelming. Using declarative language can also be helpful in getting students to talk. Educators might say, "This train looks really old to me!" to illicit responses from students telling what it is that they notice about the train.

Teachers and parents evaluate programs, and the programs are always evolving to meet the needs of their audience. In the past, teachers were given a one-page evaluation with a postage-paid envelope. There was about a 29 percent return rate of these evaluations. To increase the responses, the museum now asks teachers to write bullet points after the visits to evaluate how children are doing and progressing. They also ask parents for feedback, and the museum makes sure they are able to set different goals for each child based on the child's needs.

To create specialized programming and to provide educators with meaningful programs, the Transit Museum works with special education teachers and speech-and-language pathologists in addition to its museum educators. The museum programs are very popular, and they can expect around eight classes to come to the museum in an average week. The museum employs one educator to work with students in the fourth grade and above and another to teach prekindergarten to third grade. The museum educators generally have degrees in special education as well as museum education backgrounds.

One of the strengths of the Transit Museum for all audiences, especially children, is that the entire site is interactive; there are things to touch and climb on, and visitors can pretend to drive a bus, hand out subway tickets, and go through turnstiles. The museum even incorporates science and technology into the history through discussions of electricity and production. Through immersion in a historical environment, the Transit Museum truly teaches history and its meaning to visitors of all ages.

INTREPID SEA, AIR & SPACE MUSEUM IN NEW YORK CITY

Lori Stratton, private consultant for It Takes a Village and educator at the Intrepid Sea, Air & Space Museum, met with me in May 2012 to discuss her work with children with disabilities at museums and as a museum educator. Stratton has a degree in recreational therapy, which provides a fresh look on museum program development, and has worked in museum education at several places around New York City, including the New York City Transit Museum, where she has focused on bringing recreation therapy and history to students with special needs. Stratton's observations were particularly meaningful because of the focus on history museums and historic sites and how they can reach out to students with special needs.

Objects and artifacts are extremely powerful for telling stories; an exhibit can contain something as simple as an everyday serving platter, and from that piece, interpreters can tell stories about that time period, the people who used it, how it was made, who made it and where, how it got where it was when it was found, and countless more stories that help people build a connection with the past. As in any museum education program, Stratton thus stressed that having a tactile component is very important in history museums. Having objects, whether they are authentic or reproductions, is important to the learning process. Holding, seeing, and touching these objects helps to build connections to the past and the curriculum at hand.

Stratton also discussed the power of using popular culture in the education of children of any age; connecting to students can be as easy as finding
something to connect with them, whether it is Captain America or the movie
300. Popular culture can be a key to education with any historic site; through
brainstorming, it is possible find educational connections with superheroes,
songs, video games, television shows, or other examples relevant to particular historic sites. History museums and exhibits can also relate history to
everyday life; making connections between the past and present is one of the
best ways that students learn in informal settings.

In her time at the Transit Museum, Stratton helped to develop and present
several programs for children with special needs, especially those with autism. One program gave students paper to draw their observations; they could
draw the different types of lighting fixtures, advertisements, and seats, giving
students who are nonverbal a chance to communicate or ask questions. Another activity used photographs of the trains and a time line. The educator
used the photos to match the old and the new and put them into order. This
activity also gave students who are nonverbal the chance to express themselves and what they learned on the tour as a type of evaluative process.
Additionally, museum educators gave teachers a checklist to evaluate what
the students were learning.

When working with students with special needs at any museum, Stratton
suggested several guidelines. If a museum has eight exhibits, for example,
educators should pick only three or four to talk about and adapt the program
that day to the students' attention spans and interests. She also said that rather
than discussing specifics, educators should keep the students moving and pay
attention to their needs. In Stratton's experience, a thirty-minute program is
generally too long for a special needs audience. There can be many distractions and struggles during these programs, so educators should always remember to stay flexible and tuned in to the audience. Museums should use
spaces that are quiet and contain few visual distractions to decrease external
stimuli when speaking with a group. Ensuring that students feel as if they are
in a safe, comfortable environment will also help create a better learning
experience.

Finally, Stratton spoke about the importance of training all staff members,
not only the educators, at a museum. Security and janitorial staff must know
not to try to diagnose the children themselves and not to judge the students in
any way. All staff should know general basics of teaching children with
special needs, especially to keep calm and flexible when working with children. She suggested that educators should always remember that students
with special needs might be physically older but at a younger learning level;
she cautions educators about using programs created for younger children
with older students in secondary classes. Additionally, special education
classrooms can have various levels of learners. Museum programs should

scale down the information intellectually but still keep the program and interactions socially acceptable for any group at that age.

When educators present educational programs to children with special needs, Stratton suggested using questions that include comparison and contrast with concrete facts; an example of a question using compare and contrast could be "Is this artifact from the past or present; why do you think that?" When working with people with special needs, educators in this field must be flexible, willing to adapt to the visitors' needs, and able to allow them the opportunity to speak for themselves.

LOWER EAST SIDE TENEMENT MUSEUM IN NEW YORK CITY

The last historical site I visited in New York City was the Lower East Side Tenement Museum on Orchard Street. Sarah Litvin shared many of her experiences working as an educator at the historic site through e-mail and in person. The physical site of New York's famous tenements poses many challenges to people with physical or multiple disabilities, and the claustrophobic atmosphere within the building can also be problematic for some visitors. These challenges are typical to historic sites, and the Tenement Museum has implemented several creative alternatives to overcome these issues for their visitors with disabilities.

The Lower East Side Tenement Museum offers first-person guided tours of the historic tenement building, costumed interpretation, and walking tours for school field trips. To make the site and programs more accessible, the visitor center is much more accessible than the historic building, which is accessed via several steep stairs. Information is also shared in many different ways, including signage, audio cues, and tactile guides. They offer tours in American Sign Language and no voice interpretation during regularly scheduled public tours and school groups. For visitors with low vision, the site offers "touch tours" for groups of five or more people with advance notice. The museum does not offer specific programming for students with special needs, but it does offer modifications and flexibility for these groups. While the museum is concerned primarily with assisting visitors with low vision, hearing loss, and mobility impairments, it is working to provide more resources for visitors with autism.

The Lower East Side Tenement Museum has been a beacon within the museum world for community involvement and innovative programming. It continues to be a pioneer for history museums in reaching out to populations with disabilities. The museum tells the stories of the people who lived in the tenement building on Orchard Street on the Lower East Side of Manhattan.

The museum takes a narrative approach of interpretation for daily tours and educational groups; for instance, staff can take an object like a sewing machine and construct the stories of many people through that one artifact. In addition to other accessibility programs, the Tenement Museum offers off-site and distance learning for adults who find the museum uncomfortable or inaccessible.

Visitors may visit the museum and historic building only by taking a guided tour of the building. The museum offers many specialized tours, including *Hard Times*, *Sweatshop Workers*, *Irish Outsiders*, and *Exploring 97 Orchard Street*. It also offers school group tours and community involvement opportunities.[13] Tours generally begin with the group walking up the steps of the tenement at 97 Orchard Street into a dark hall. The tour group then climbs the steps, holding onto the original banister that so many people in the past have held before. Many apartments were used not only for living but also for operating the family's garment industry shops and other businesses. Visitors view primary documents related to the neighborhood, garment industry, and reforms and also look at the artifacts and furnishings that were typical of tenement family rooms.

Figure 4.5.   The Lower East Side Tenement Museum talking tactile tablet

Standing in the same building where people lived and worked in the past, looking at the artifacts they used each day, and hearing the sounds outside the tenement can evoke feelings that would not be possible to experience in another location. Without getting people with mobility or other impairments into the physical space, how can museums provide the same experience?

The accessibility section of the museum website offers touch tours for people with sight impairments and sign language tours for people with hearing impairments. The orientation film is captioned for those with hearing impairments, and Braille and large-print versions of primary sources, which are shown throughout the tour, are also available on request. [14]

Additionally, at the time of this visit to the visitor center, the Accessible Learning Center included a talking tablet and a tablet with a raised façade of the main building and floor plans for people with sight impairments to "see" the layout and size of the rooms within the tenement building (see figure 4.5).

The historic building offers many challenges to people with disabilities, especially those with physical disabilities or difficulties. As mentioned above, several steep steps to the door offer the only entrance to the tenement building, and once inside the building, visitors encounter the original, old wooden staircase, which must be traversed to experience the guided tour.

The website offers other opportunities for those using wheelchairs or other implements, including a new exhibit that opened in 2012 called *Shop Life*, which explores the many businesses housed at 97 Orchard Street. It is the museum's first ever wheelchair-accessible exhibit at the site. *Tour the Neighborhood* is wheelchair accessible, and during the winter, *Foods of the Lower East Side* is held in an accessible room. Additionally, the visitor center has universally designed elevators and restrooms on the ground level. There is also a "virtual tour" that benefits not only people with disabilities who cannot visit the historic building but really anyone who wants to experience the site without a visit to New York City. [15]

Litvin shared some examples of success and failure in the development of programs for children with special needs, the most important being to create object-based programs. When working with many special needs groups, especially children with autism, setting an agenda or schedule of the program's events can help ease discomfort among students. One way the museum attempted to provide stress relief and focus for students was through the use of stress balls on which students could concentrate their energy. The stress balls were printed with an object from the collections to focus questions and ideas while touring the historic site. There were some logistical problems with the stress balls, but the museum staff members are working on preparing more options. Museum educators also provide notebooks or sketchbooks as a visual option for students to communicate. The children can use the notebook to sketch things that they think are important to focus their questions and energies. Educators try to talk to the teacher before the visit to evaluate the students' needs. Museum educators also have a checklist of behaviors that they review before visits to know what tactics might work with the scheduled student groups.

As with every other site, training of sensitivity and awareness of all staff members is imperative to the staff at the Lower East Side Tenement Museum. Litvin shared that "every new staff member has Access Awareness training as part of their initial Museum orientation. Follow-up and additional training is available for staff as well."[16] In addition, at least two access workshops are held at the museum for all staff to learn more about specific issues.

SMITHSONIAN INSTITUTION MUSEUMS IN WASHINGTON, DC

Krista Flores from the Smithsonian Institution Accessibility Program discussed with me how the Smithsonian is creating special events for families with children on the autism spectrum. "Mornings at the Museum" is available for this population to visit the museum a half hour before it is open to the general public; this special time eliminates many distractions that children may face during the busiest part of the day at the museum. The staff lowers the light level for the children and starts with only one exhibit at a time to create a more soothing environment. Previsit materials called "social stories" are also available for the parents of children on the autism spectrum to share with their children before they visit the museum.[17]

Carol Gray, author of social stories for the Smithsonian Institution, explains that the materials describe a situation, skill, or concept in terms of relevant social cues, perspectives, and common responses in a patient and reassuring manner that the audience easily understands.[18] These web-based materials include information about crowd control, what to expect in the galleries, acceptable behaviors at a museum, and sensory maps to explain where in the exhibit there are interactive elements or displays that light up or make sounds. These materials have made it possible for parents to feel more comfortable bringing their children to the museum and also provide the children with an agenda of what to expect to keep their stimulation at a lower level.

Using these programs as models, other museums can create programs that are accessible to groups of any age or ability. The most successful steps that one can take in designing these programs are outlined in the following chapter.

NOTES

1. Museum Access Consortium, http://www.cityaccessny.org/mac.php (accessed March 15, 2013).

2. One of the main reasons I chose New York City as my research hub was the concentration of museums, and the citizens of the metro area value and support museums to a greater extent than in many other areas of the country. The MAC website led me to several different museum websites, where I was able to learn about programs available to people with special needs. Employees came from the Museum of Modern Art; the New York City Metro Transit Museum; the Intrepid Sea, Air & Space Museum; and the Lower East Side Tenement Museum. It is important to note that, of the museums visited, the Museum of Modern Art is an institute dedicated to art, and the Transit, Intrepid, and Tenement Museums are museums centered on history.

3. Museum of Modern Art, "Meet Me at MoMA," http://www.moma.org/meetme/index (accessed April 4, 2013).

4. All comments are from participants in the "Meet Me at MoMA" program from May 8, 2012.

5. For more information about this piece and its use in the "Meet Me at MoMA" program, see http://www.moma.org/meetme/modules/module_one#module_1_1 (accessed April 4, 2013).

6. For more information about the painting and its use in the program, see Museum of Modern Art, "Meet Me at MoMA," http://www.moma.org/meetme/modules/module_one#module_1_3 (accessed April 4, 2013).

7. These statements were made by participants in the "Meet Me at MoMA" group.

8. See Museum of Modern Art, "Meet Me at MoMA," http://www.moma.org/meetme/modules/ module_two#module_2_4 (accessed April 4, 2013).

9. Notes from the Southeastern Museums Conference session, October 9, 2013.

10. Jacksonville Museum of Contemporary Art, "Rainbow Artists," http://www.mocajacksonville.org/community/rainbow (accessed December 1, 2013).

11. Notes from the Southeastern Museums Conference session.

12. Interview by author, New York, May 10, 2012.

13. Tenement Museum, "Visit: Tours and Tickets," http://www.tenement.org/tours.php (accessed April 4, 2013).

14. Tenement Museum, "Visit: Accessibility," http://www.tenement.org/vizinfo_ada.html (accessed April 4, 2013).

15. Lower East Side Tenement Museum, "Virtual Tour," http://www.tenement.org/VirtualTour/index_virtual.html (accessed April 4, 2013).

16. Sarah Litvin, e-mail interview by author, April 2013.

17. More information about "social stories" and examples are available at Smithsonian Institution, "Morning at the Museum: Social Stories," http://accessible.si.edu/MATM/social-stories.html (accessed April 4, 2013).

18. Smithsonian Institution, "Morning at the Museum."

Chapter Five

A Case Study and Model for Museums and Historic Sites

Seven Key Elements of Effective Programs

This chapter explores the process of creating educational programming for children with special needs and the elements that go into successful programs at any museum or historic site. The case study took place at the Sam Davis Home and Museum, a Civil War–era historic site in Smyrna, Tennessee. The programs presented in previous chapters influenced this process and inspired me to create a model for museums to adapt for their own sites.

Smyrna is a town in Rutherford County, Tennessee, approximately twenty miles southeast of Nashville. The population is approximately 40,000, and the Sam Davis Home is the only historic site in the town. The Sam Davis Home and Museum has a senior staff of two full-time employees, including an executive director and education coordinator, and a part-time events coordinator. There are also five tour guides or docents who regularly work onsite. The budget of this museum is typical of other historic house museums in the region. The property includes 160 acres with a historic house; several slave cabins; outbuildings that include a smokehouse, kitchen, and outhouse; and the Boyhood Home, where Sam Davis was born.

The first step in this process was to contact schools, districts, and online communities for assistance and suggestions for a focus group. The process began with an online survey; next came distributing the survey through e-mail listservs, online forums, college class lists, and social media. [1] Working with the public directly in the community that the museum serves is essential to successful programming; staff should contact teachers and advocate groups in their area for assistance. Important questions to ask in the preliminary stage include the following: Where do students currently go on field trips, if they take trips? What types of disabilities are represented in your classroom? What do you hope to get out of a field trip? and What types of programs would your students benefit from?

The eighteen teachers surveyed for this research project represented educators from Tennessee, Illinois, Ohio, Virginia, Kentucky, South Carolina, Pennsylvania, Mississippi, and Ontario, Canada. The surveyed teachers work with a variety of age ranges in the classroom, from prekindergarten to adults. The survey (figure 5.1) showed that 14 percent teach prekindergarten students, 27 percent teach kindergarten to second grade, 9 percent teach third to fifth grade, 14 percent teach sixth to eighth grade, and 27 percent teach secondary classes of ninth to twelfth grade. The ages of children in the community can determine the field trips and the sites visited on field trips. Prekindergarten students would be less likely to visit historic sites, as museums rarely serve that age range at many museums, children's museums being exceptions.

The next—and one of the most important—questions asked teachers if and where they take students on field trips. Of those surveyed (figure 5.2), twelve teachers, or 66.7 percent, responded that they do take their students on a field trip each year. Two teachers (11.1 percent) do not take students on field trips, and five teachers (27.8 percent) sometimes take students on a field trip in the academic year. The survey also explored the types of field trips that teachers take their students on, and the survey results showed that parks were the most popular destination among those surveyed. Science museums and none of the above tied for second, as 15 percent of teachers either visit science museums or take no field trips. Historical sites garnered 14 percent of the teachers surveyed, and 12 percent of teachers selected art museums as a destination. Teachers also listed children's museums, history museums, aquariums, and live theater as field trip locations.

In the initial survey (figure 5.3), each teacher answered what kinds of disabilities they see in their classrooms. Teachers listed as many disabilities as they desired, and some listed specific disabilities, while others gave general answers. The spectrum of disabilities varied, and some teachers listed physical disabilities and others behavioral, emotional, or learning disabilities. This variation is representative of many classrooms for children with special needs. Almost any classroom from any age-group will contain a variety of children with different needs, so the variety of disabilities should come as no surprise.

Teachers expressed that they want their students to gain social, educational, and life skills from field trips. One teacher commented, "I believe real-life experiences are highly important. They need to know how to survive. Someone may not always be there for them. They need to know other things outside of the home." A smaller number of teachers also included behavioral

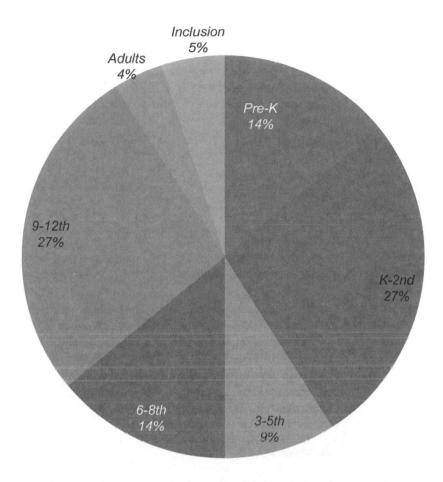

Figure 5.1. Grades of special education students of surveyed teachers

skills and responsibility as attributes they like their students to gain on field trips. Teachers also listed enjoyment and experiences equal to other students.

Because education outside of the classroom is not always included in standardized testing, teachers expressed that they evaluate the learning that takes place in separate environments in a variety of ways. Observation was the evaluative tool for 40 percent, while 25 percent use discussion with their students to determine what students learned on a field trip. Twenty percent of teachers selected enthusiasm as a measurable outcome, while 5 percent chose student behavior, written evaluation, and student performance.

One of the most important questions asked in the survey was, "What kinds of museum programs would you like for your students to participate in?" (figure 5.5). Teachers want to experience programs with educational

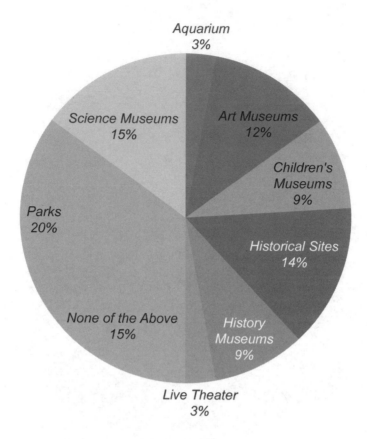

Figure 5.2.   Special education students field trips

content, hands-on activities, and entertaining approaches. Tactile and hands-on programs are among the most successful and popular programs at most museums among all visitors, and children with special needs are no exception.

Other important questions in this study were, "What would you need, as a teacher, to feel comfortable taking your students on a field trip to a museum?" and "What would your students need, and would a field trip to a museum be something you consider worth your and the students' time?" These answers helped to shape programs that would be desirable to both the students and the teachers.

Answers included the following:

- Proper transportation with chair lifts, etc., funding for the trips since a lot of our kids cannot afford them, administrative support.
- Hands-on artworks and encourage the students to touch the statues.

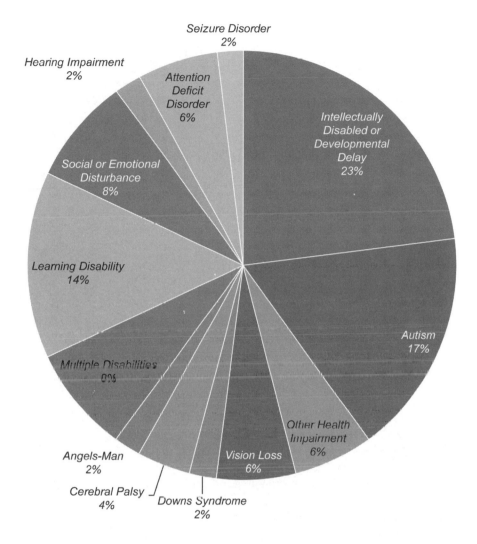

Figure 5.3.   Types of disability in surveyed classroom

- One-on-one adult with my particular students. I would love to take them anywhere and let them experience anything I could.
- Knowing that there is at least one thing every student can participate in.
- The trouble is financing . . . busing, costs, etc.
- Yes. They may need a teacher assistant to go with them.
- Access for wheelchairs, a place to change incontinent students if needed.
- Yes, but financial considerations usually prohibit this type of field trip.
- Hands-on exhibits very important.

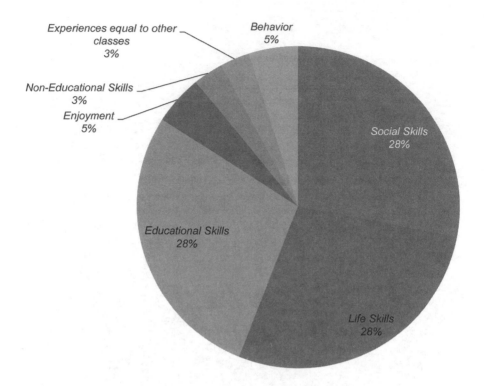

Figure 5.4.   Desired learning experience from field trip

- As long as I had one other person to help me make sure the kids are acting appropriately, I would feel comfortable. I think my students would only need a familiar teacher with them.
- Accommodations for children with motor impairments, access to information beforehand.
- We need to bring enough chaperones, lunch, and sometimes books to read while on the bus.
- More parental involvement; museums might be okay to go to, but children are a little young (unless it's the children's museum, especially for preschoolers).
- I would need to feel that my students were trustworthy enough. Students would need to be in groups and, maybe, museum personnel lead.
- I would want the museum to be child friendly and interactive. I would want bathroom facilities to be available to children who need assistance with them or other occupants of the restroom feeling uncomfortable. It would be helpful to have the exits to the building supervised so that if a child gets away, the exits are protected.

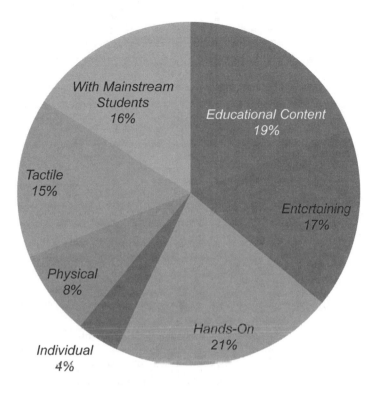

Figure 5.5. Educator preferences for programs

- Yes, field trips to local and more metropolitan areas to take in museums would be beneficial. Adequate chaperones and previsits would be beneficial for staff. Students would benefit from pretaught background information/layouts/expectations.
- One capable and able adult per child. My students would need an accessible bathroom with a changing area, as all but one are in diapers. We would also need a quiet area for students, some with severe autism, to have if they are having difficulty with sensory overload. I would love to take my students to a small local museum to see the dinosaur exhibit or to the children's museum.

A troubling answer to this question stated, "I don't think I'd consider anything other than a natural history museum . . . a docent with ability/willingness to depart from usual 'canned' speech and interact." This statement shows the notion that many people still have of the history museum as a quiet, boring place with docents who have no flexibility or willingness to participate with students.

Most teachers express that financial constraints prevent them from taking field trips and that physical access for students is a concern in many places. The lack of parents and chaperones to accompany the group is also a problem. Again, answers mentioned the need for hands-on opportunities for students as well as a friendly environment for the students. Some teachers worry that students will misbehave on the field trip or that students will not be safe, as there may be several exits for students to leave. Previsit information, such as schedules, maps, or handouts of what students can expect would be a great addition to any museum information packet, as some teachers mentioned.

SAM DAVIS HOME AND MUSEUM SITE VISITS

To create a model program based on a trip to the Sam Davis Home and Museum in Smyrna, Tennessee, a secondary school special education class visited the museum twice. A special educator from the Rutherford County school system brought her class of high school students from the Transition Academy, which helps students from special education classes prepare for the workforce. In this group, the students were all verbal, and none used mobility devices.

The teacher received a previsit survey to assess the needs of the teachers and students when they were on the site. She observed, "Most of my students have previously been to the Sam Davis Home. We talk about what they already know about Sam Davis and the tour, the sequence of events for the day, when and how to ask appropriate questions, and appropriate attire for the day."[2] The educator said that her students were most looking forward to doing "things out of their routine and to be outside." Students who had previously visited the site were excited to visit the historic house again. She shared that she hoped her students would "gain knowledge about the history of the area they live in, be aware of how things have changed, ask appropriate questions when necessary, and learn to respect artifacts, presenters, buildings, etc."

The only thing the special educator mentioned that she was apprehensive about was that "some of the students have been to the Sam Davis Home as a job site. Sometimes it is difficult for them to differentiate between guest and worker." Through the Transition Academy, many students worked at the Sam Davis Home in the past to get experience working in a public environment.

With this information from the lead classroom teacher and the knowledge that twelve students would be at the site along with four teachers, I worked with the staff at the Sam Davis Home to plan the visit. The education coordinator at the museum, Rebecca Duke, and I decided that the Sam Davis Home would plan for this visit independently to provide an experience for the school group that would be typical for any field trip to the site.

Most groups that visit the Sam Davis Home go on a basic tour of the historic house and outbuildings, watch the orientation video to the site, walk through the museum, and participate in one or two educational programs, such as "Life under the Gun" or "Seasons on the Farm," that the teachers choose. Tour guides are responsible for the content of these activities, but the educational coordinator works with the teacher to find out the students' needs and the educators' wants from the field trip.

On November 2, 2012, a group of twelve students, four teachers and aides, and one classroom intern arrived at the Sam Davis Home. The field trip began with a welcome from Duke and an introductory film about the historic site and the family that lived there.

After the fifteen-minute introductory video, the students began a scavenger hunt around the museum. Duke explained the instructions and divided the students into three groups with four students and a teacher in each group. In addition to explaining the instructions to the worksheet, Duke made sure that the students knew that in a museum there is no handling of the artifacts. The scavenger hunt consisted of ten questions about the museum hall exhibits. A copy of this scavenger hunt is included in appendix C. Duke then stepped back, as with all school groups, to allow the teachers and students to complete the scavenger hunt independently. If a teacher or student had a question, they could certainly ask, but this is largely an autonomous activity.

Observation of this activity noted that many of the students did have the ability to read, though in many cases the teachers would help the students find the answers by helping to read the questions on the worksheet and guiding students to the proper exhibit in which to find the answer. For example, a question involved the name "Gracey"; the teacher helped the students by saying, "Look for 'Gracey'; it starts with a 'G.'"

Once all students were finished, Duke went through the answers to make sure all the groups successfully completed the hunt. She then asked students about their favorite and least favorite things at the museum and what they learned in the exhibits. Morgan explained that even though many students had been through the museum before, they had not learned as much as they did with the scavenger hunt because this time they were engaged in an activity that required them to read and investigate the exhibits.

Next, the students went into the conference room in the visitor center to take part in the educational program "Life under the Gun." The interpreter presented the program, which provides a lecture and observation of artifacts that relate to students what it would have been like to have been a soldier during the Civil War. The Sam Davis Home website describes the program:

Did Civil War soldiers have toothbrushes? What did the soldiers do when they weren't fighting? Students will discover through common items carried by the soldiers on both sides what life was like in a Civil War camp. Uniforms and equipment from both armies are presented for examination in this hands-on program.[3]

Observations suggested that while many of the students were engaged in the program, more engagement and hands-on opportunities would have been beneficial. When the interpreter passed around objects from the program, the students were able to see, touch, and feel the historical artifacts, sparking questions and conversation; if more objects were passed around rather than just shown from the front of the room, perhaps students would be more engaged and retain more information from the program. Rather than a simple lecture while showing objects, more questions could also provide more engagement and thoughtfulness among the students. For instance, one of the objects used in the program is a haversack filled with items that a soldier may have carried while marching, including a potato, apple, peanuts, a mending kit, a corncob, and a pipe. The interpreter could easily pass these items among students to engage them and provide a chance for conversation about why soldiers would carry those items, how soldiers used the items, and how that compares with current soldiers.

After the program, the teachers and students requested an unplanned bathroom break. In the future, bathroom breaks should be included in the planning process, not just for groups with special needs but also for all groups. Following the program, the group went to the historic house, outbuildings, and grounds for a tour by education coordinator Rebecca Duke. Students seemed to enjoy themselves, but again the tour could incorporate more engagement with questions and conversation throughout.

Immediately after the visit, all teachers present received a survey to evaluate their experiences at the Sam Davis Home and Museum. All four educators participated in the survey. Results show that three participants were "very satisfied" with the "Life under the Gun" program, while one was "somewhat satisfied." When asked how the program could be improved, there were no suggestions from the survey results. All were "very satisfied" with their instructor from the Sam Davis Home for the program. One educator commented, "It was great to have the artifacts passed around. I also loved the questions asked of the group; it really got them involved and required them to focus. Lots of these kids have no idea about history. Maybe start off by asking what they would pack for a long trip or journey."

Three teachers rated the house tour as "somewhat satisfied," while one rated it as "very satisfied." To improve the house tour, educators suggested that the guide could have told more stories, visited more of the outbuildings, explained in more detail, and asked engaging questions of the students. For example, one educator gave examples of such questions: "If you had to go to the bathroom in the middle of the night, what would you do? What kinds of things are in your bedroom? Do you have to share a room?" Two teachers rated the interpreter as "somewhat satisfied," while two others marked "very satisfied." Suggestions for improvements to the house tour included no rushing through, giving more information, and, again, asking more questions. Another participant praised the interpreter for giving a good amount of information.

Each educator gave a different answer to the question "What did your students enjoy the most about the field trip?" Answers included the scavenger hunt, the tour of the home, everything, and "The girls seemed to like the house tour and the boys liked [the education interpreter]." When asked what the students least enjoyed, the answers were nothing, "Maybe the scavenger hunt could have had a reward," "None," and "They were hungry at the end (not much you can do about that)."

An important question to this study was, "What challenges did you face, as a teacher and chaperone, on this field trip and at the Sam Davis Home?" Three teachers answered, "None," and another teacher had a more descriptive answer. She wrote:

> Helping the students to find the answers to the scavenger hunt was difficult. I LOVE the scavenger hunt. The nonreaders had a very difficult time locating and recognizing the answers. It would have helped me to know ahead of time that they were going to be in groups so I could have assigned the nonreaders to be with one or two readers.

A question about what students learned on their trip also provided answers helpful to the evaluation of the study. Two answered that the students learned about history and the site, and another answered that students learned about Sam Davis and his family. The other participant said that there was a significant impact on students with the ways life was different in the past and how war can affect a family.

To improve the tour for the next time, the survey asked teachers, "What tips do you have for making your students' next trip to the Sam Davis Home a more successful and enjoyable experience?" Two had no suggestions. One answered, "More history on the home, maybe folktales of things that have happened. Something to keep them more entertained and focused." Another said, "Scavenger hunt was a good idea, but not if the students can't read a modified scavenger hunt." Three educators rated their trip "very satisfied," while one was "somewhat satisfied."

As museum staff and I planned the next field trip with the group, these survey answers were invaluable. Students on the second field trip to the Sam Davis Home participated in the "Seasons on the Farm" educational program, which is an outdoor scavenger hunt; a revisit to the museum with a modified scavenger hunt; and a house tour. Many of the students were on the same field trip as the last group, but there were some new students.

Executive Director of the Sam Davis Home in 2012, Meredith Baughman, received training related to sensitivity and awareness before providing the interpretation. Baughman worked from a compilation of comments from the survey after the November visit, and I also shared ideas and tips from the national survey with her. Baughman previously worked with special needs children, which was a useful experience for this program.

The students arrived on March 8, 2012, and Baughman welcomed the students in the museum theater. A bathroom break was scheduled for this time, so while waiting for all students to arrive, Baughman asked students what they remembered from their last visit and what they enjoyed the most. Once all students were present, Baughman went through the schedule of the morning with them and then gave instructions for their first activity: a modified museum scavenger hunt.

Because the students had already visited the museum, Sam Davis Home and Museum staff changed the scavenger hunt to accommodate their learning needs. The staff and teachers divided students into four groups of three students, with one teacher per group. The students traveled through the museum, with each group starting in a different gallery. Baughman asked the students to explore the museum, and she tasked each group with finding three things in the museum that they did not see on their previous visit. This activity required the use of cognitive recall and creativity as well. The museum scavenger hunt focused on such specific artifacts, so this activity allowed the students to choose items in the museum that caught their attention.

A major difference from the students' last visit was a new exhibit, *Women's History*, focused on the women of the Davis plantation, including the sisters, mother, and grandmother of Sam Davis in addition to the enslaved workers from the 1860 census. Many students were enthralled with items in this display, but the item that acquired the most appreciation was the braided hair specimen from one of the women, Andromedia Davis Matthews, who lived on the plantation in the nineteenth century.

While students went throughout the museum in search of intriguing artifacts, Baughman circulated throughout the galleries to answer questions and engage students by calling attention to specific things that are of interest to her and many other visitors. While students in one group explored the *Women's History* exhibit, Baughman asked who among the students had the longest hair. They then made a comparison of the length and discussed the differences of hairstyles between the mid-nineteenth century and today.

Once the students had a chance to tour the exhibits and find something new, they all gathered in the museum theater to discuss their answers. Many students said that they were impressed with Andromedia's hair, and a discussion with the entire class about the similarities and differences occurred. Another student mentioned that he was impressed with the blacksmith artifacts. He then explained to the class how people in the past used the items, and the class discussed how different manufacturing is today.

Students were very curious about the temporary exhibit, and Baughman took the opportunity to explain why some items reside in curatorial storage while others remain in the museum or in the historic house on display. Baughman told the class about light, humidity, and temperature and how they can damage artifacts if they are not properly controlled. Students commented that the theater was brighter than the exhibit galleries because there are no artifacts housed there. The students also learned how oils from their hands could damage certain artifacts, which is why the objects are behind protective glass. This portion of the lesson was an addition from the last time, and it helped the students understand why the architects constructed the museum that way and gave context to the rules that are inherent within museums.

Before the group left the museum, Baughman again reinforced the schedule so that students would be prepared for the rest of the morning and feel comfortable. Following the visit to the museum galleries, students went on a tour of the property and historic buildings. The tour route was different this time; instead of focusing mainly on the house, Baughman took the students by the barn, fields, and slave cabins before touring the historic house (see figure 5.6). This path gave Baughman the opportunity to ask more questions about farm life, animals that would have been on the farm in the past, and the slaves who lived on the site. Baughman used inquiry throughout the tour, asking such questions as "How did people farm in the past, and how is that different than today?" and "Where did the Davis family get their food?" She was able to relate the history to modern students' lives by comparing and contrasting to the Davis family.

The tour that Baughman presented was more in depth than on the previous field trip, and the students had more opportunity for questions. Relying on the results of the teacher survey from the last visit, Baughman also told more stories about specific people and objects, which engaged the students. For instance, Baughman pointed out that the bricks the students walked on were made on the site, and she showed them a certain brick in the chimney that had a toe print on it (see figure 5.7). This example humanized the people who made the bricks and lived 150 years ago, and the students seemed impressed that a permanent record of the person who made the brick was present still today.

Baughman continued her inquiry and narrative-based tour throughout the historic house, and she made a comparison of the main house to the Boyhood Home cabin and the slave cabins. Once inside the house, the guide attracted attention to the fact that it was cold in the house, and students commented

Figure 5.6.   Baughman leading the class on a modified tour route by the slave cabins

that it was very different from the museum. They also expressed concern for the artifacts in the house since they were not in a controlled environment, which showed their understanding of the short lesson in the museum earlier in the morning. Although the house is cold today, Baughman pointed out, when the Davis family lived there, they would have used fire for heat and light. Students first looked in the formal parlor, and Baughman asked them how it was different from rooms in their homes. Students answered that there was no television, no outlets or electricity, and no radio systems.

The students explained to Baughman, rather than the guide telling the students, that the Davis family used candles instead of electricity. The inquiry-based tour continued, and Baughman told stories and related the history back to the students' lives. One of the students' favorite stories was the explanation of the saying "Sleep tight, don't let the bed bugs bite," which comes from tightening of rope beds and the plethora of insects that lived in mattress stuffing in the past. Teachers commented that the tour guide on the house tour was doing a great job and that the students seemed engaged (see figure 5.9).

Figure 5.7.   Baughman shows students a toe print left in a brick

Outside once again, the students visited the kitchen and the smokehouse. Baughman invited one of the students to ring the kitchen bell, and they discussed what the bell was used for and how loud it was. The guide explained the use of many contraptions exhibited in the kitchen and told students that the meat of over 200 hogs would fit in the smokehouse. The tour continued by the herb garden and the cemetery, which students remembered from the last visit, and finally the students were led back to the museum for a bathroom break and to begin their outdoor scavenger hunt, "Seasons on the Farm."

Figure 5.8.   Baughman explains how an iron was used during the nineteenth century

For the "Seasons on the Farm" scavenger hunt, Baughman and the teachers placed students in four groups of three students, with one teacher per group. The program focuses on the different seasons and the chores and work that happened on a plantation during each season. The scavenger hunt takes groups across the grounds from fields and slave cabins to the herb garden and in view of Stewart's Creek. Each station represents a season and the chores that took place on that site; for example, the cotton fields represent winter, when slaves harvested crops. On completing the scavenger hunt, the groups came together again and discussed their findings. Baughman also asked the students which season they thought would be the hardest, and most replied that the harvest, fall and winter, was the most difficult. They then related chores in the past to those that they are responsible for at their own homes.

To accommodate the teachers' requests in the survey from the November visit, Baughman added a hands-on activity to the field trip schedule. The visitor center houses an object table, which includes many artifacts that date from the nineteenth century, including a cannonball, a curling iron, a candle mold, and lye soap. Baughman presented each object to the students, and

Figure 5.9. A student rings the kitchen bell while everyone covers their ears

rather than telling students what the artifact was, she asked the students to think about the item and come to their own conclusions (figure 5.10).

After Baughman and the students discussed each item, students passed the object around and were able to touch and see it firsthand. Because in the past the plantation grew cotton primarily, each student was given a piece of cotton to see how difficult it is to get the seeds and dirt out of the fiber, and each of the students took home a cotton bole. This activity, as well as the entire visit, seemed to be a great success. At the end of the activities, one student exclaimed, "I learned so much my brain is turning to mush!"

After the visit, teachers submitted their comments and rated the trip through an online survey. All three participating teachers rated the "Seasons on the Farm" program as "very satisfied." One teacher mentioned that the students and teachers enjoyed it more than the scavenger hunt that students participated in on their last trip, and no teachers had any suggestions for improvement of the program for their students. Similarly, all three teachers rated the grounds and house tour as "very satisfied" with no suggestions for improvements of the interpretation. Teachers also rated the interpreter, Baughman, very highly, and teachers described her as informative and enthusiastic; one teacher wrote that she "couldn't have been better."[4]

Figure 5.10. **Baughman demonstrating a nineteenth-century curling iron**

Each teacher responded differently to the question "What did your students enjoy the most about the field trip?" One teacher said that "Seasons on the Farm" was the most popular, while another answered that the tour of the grounds and the historic house was the most enjoyable to students. Another teacher claimed that the students loved everything. When asked what students enjoyed the least, all three teachers agreed that the students liked the entire trip and that they did not complain about any aspect. The survey also asked about any challenges the teachers faced on the trip, and all responded that they were satisfied and had no problems.

The teachers also responded that, based on their observations and from talking to the students, they believed that the students learned more from this field trip than the previous one. In particular, they learned more about the house, slaves, and specific artifacts. One teacher said, "It was interesting which facts different students absorbed . . . [those facts] varied from realizing that Sam Davis was hung to what cotton looks like."[5] Another teacher said that the "Seasons on the Farm" scavenger hunt helped students retain knowledge through recall during the program. Overall, all three teachers rated their satisfaction with the trip as "very satisfied." Teachers mentioned the level of detail and tactile components as positives in comparison to the last trip.

Baughman was excited to share her experiences with the students. She commented that it was very encouraging to see that the students were excited about the property and the history. She enjoyed answering the students' questions and even looked in the archives to answer some more specific questions before the students left. She said there were some differences between this group and other tours that she has led, mostly because it was a new way of interpreting the past to the public. The tour that Baughman gave to the group provided more interaction and inquiry between the guide and the visitors. She felt that this led to better interpretation because the visitors thought for themselves instead of listening to a lecture. They were provided with the opportunity to formulate questions that they would not been told the answers to otherwise.

Baughman said, "I didn't know what to expect, so I was nervous in the beginning, but they were excited and receptive." She said her favorite part of the whole experience was talking about slavery and how hard the slaves' lives were; the students were interested, and you could see that they understood something new that they had not learned on the last trip. She particularly enjoyed this because she "could visibly see acknowledgment of a history they hadn't understood before." Because the historic site has historic slave cabins on the site, students could see where the slaves lived in small cabins and the insides of those homes. Baughman said, "When I explained that there were fifty-one slaves and fourteen cabins, you could see the students doing the math in their heads that so many people lived in a room the size of their bedroom at home."

The Sam Davis Home and Museum staff hopes to continue to offer this type of programming to school groups that visit the site. The staff has not yet implemented a system to reach out to students and their teachers; however, students with special needs already participate in a work-study program there, so networking with teachers will not be difficult. Museum staff could also use advertising programs through newsletters, social media, and e-mail lists of teachers and area schools.

SEVEN ELEMENTS OF EFFECTIVE PROGRAMS

As the case studies from the New York City Transit Museum, the Museum of Modern Art, the Sam Davis Home, and others clearly indicate, visitors with intellectual disabilities can have an enriching experience at museums when educators combine effective exhibits and universal design environments with object-centered education techniques and inquiry methods of teaching. The model for programming at historic sites and museums meets the needs of people with intellectual disabilities and other cognitive or developmental delays. Historic sites and museums can implement universally designed programs for all audiences with disabilities by following several key steps (see table 5.1).

As the surveys, discussions with museum professionals, and practical experiences show, sensitivity and awareness training for all staff members make up one of the most important and universal elements when addressing the needs of people with disabilities. This training is one of the first steps in

Table 5.1. Seven Key Components to Create Programs for Audiences with Disabilities at Historic Sites and Museums

	Key Concept	Purpose
1	Sensitivity and awareness training	Training is essential for museum staff to be aware of techniques to provide a safe and welcoming environment.
2	Planning and communication	Planning and communication is essential to prepare the staff, educators, and visitors so they know what to expect at the site.
3	Timing	Each segment of the visit should be no longer than thirty minutes. This provides the opportunity to ask questions and learn about a certain topic, but it is not so prolonged that visitors lose interest.
4	Engagement	Interacting with docents and also other visitors at the museums can help with social and life skills.
5	Object centered and inquiry based	Physical connections to the past and asking questions engage visitors more than a general lecture or demonstration.
6	Structure	An agenda or schedule is important for the staff and visitors to stay on task and accomplish all educational goals.
7	Flexibility	Interpreters should be able to adapt to the needs of the visitors and their interests and abilities.

creating programs and welcoming populations with disabilities. Staff education should be incorporated into the training programs of all museums and historic sites, when feasible, to provide a safe and welcoming environment for all visitors regardless of ability.

The first staff members with whom a visitor comes into contact at a museum or historic site are the most important; the first impression determines the overall feeling of comfort that a visitor has while there. Security guards, cashiers, and greeters are essential personnel that need to have the training to work with any audience.

Personal awareness is the first step to working with any group of people, and staff should be prepared to communicate with and assist any visitor who comes to the site. Chapter 2 references several training materials and techniques that museum administrators can adapt for their own museums and staff. Managers should attend workshops, conferences, and other professional development opportunities to learn about current trends and solutions. Museums may even consider creating events or public programs that provide awareness and sensitivity information to the surrounding community.

Another key element is effective planning. To ensure that a site is serving visitors, teachers, and students successfully, communication with the visitors is essential both before and after field trips. Contacting teachers or group leaders before the visit prepares the staff, museum educators, teachers, and students and lets all individuals involved know what to expect. By communicating effectively, the museum staff can learn what student and teacher needs are while on the site; additionally, the staff can inform the teacher of any important information related to the field trip. Once the staff are aware of any special needs or accommodations, they can properly prepare for the most effective programs without many surprises.

With any museum program, reaching out to the audience after a visit ensures that visitors can express any comments or suggestions after the visit for incorporation into future visits. Surveys or interviews show what visitors learned, enjoyed, or found challenging. The results of surveys can help with future groups and serve as a training tool for museum staff. Evaluations of programs before, after, and during the time they take place are some of the most important aspects of educational development at museums.

Effective timing is a third key component. Generally, each segment of the program should be no longer than thirty minutes per section. For example, at the Sam Davis Home and Museum, the class experienced thirty minutes per session in the museum, on the property and outbuildings of the site, in the historic house, doing the "Seasons on the Farm" scavenger hunt, and working through the object table. This amount of time gives the visitors the opportunity to ask questions and learn about a certain topic, but the program is not so prolonged that visitors lose interest. Also important is the time of day or night when the program takes place; for example, if the museum is busiest with general public visitors at a certain time, perhaps the museum should schedule the program during a slower time of business to accommodate spatial and staff needs.

A fourth key component involves strategies of engagement, meeting multiple needs of the audience. The nationwide survey of special education teachers showed that while educational aspects are integral to museum field trips, social and life skills are important as well. Interacting with tour guides and docents and other visitors at museums can help with these benchmarks for students. Almost any visitor prefers the personal touch of learning at his or her own pace about topics of interest to the individual. Inquiry-based tours or programs provide a personal learning experience tailored to the specific visitor.

Moreover, allowing the audience to "touch" the past through object-centered instruction becomes a fifth key component, especially when used in tandem with inquiry-based interpretations, as Baughman used at the Sam Davis Home and Museum. Relating to visitors through physical connections to the past engages the student more than a general lecture or demonstration. Additionally, historic structures provide a space outside the realm of modern museums or school buildings, forging a connection between the past and today that is tangible. Primary sources, photographs, artifacts, and spaces can show the similarities and differences between the past and today that one cannot get through text or basic interpretive information.

A general structure or agenda of the program events is important for the staff and students to stay on task and accomplish all educational goals. However, perhaps the most important characteristic that museum staff should have is flexibility to adapt to the needs of the students. As the interpreters or educators move throughout the activities, they should be able to adapt to the group's interests and abilities. Structure can provide the framework and plan, which many people find comforting, especially in a new or strange setting.

Flexibility is essential in any museum work, as many staff members know. Many sites today remain understaffed or underfunded, leading to a diverse group of job descriptions. A day in the life of a museum employee can range from tracking through a muddy field to climbing in a historic, dusty attic or from sitting in front of a computer working through curriculum standards to writing grants to fund educational programs. Because of this reality, the ideal employee of a museum or historic site is intrinsically flexible throughout the workday. Staff should apply this ability to programs at all times, especially when working with children.

Rather than creating an entire new curriculum to serve students with special needs or visitors with a range of disabilities at museums and historic sites, staff can adapt existing programs and tours incorporating more inquiry and engagement and modifying language and content to the learning level of the classes. Communication with the teachers or group leaders to determine appropriate subjects and student learning levels related to the material is essential to meeting the students' needs. The staff should use observation and evaluation of successes and failures to know what works and what does not work at individual sites.

Essentially, as proponents of universal design have taught us, museum professionals should use all of these best practices for working with students in any school group. All ages and learning levels seem to learn more from engagement and inquiry-based learning, and people enjoy this technique more than listening to a lecture, as in a classroom.

Many obstacles still exist for educators to create inclusive museums and historic sites. Historic sites have many specific difficulties because they are tangibly inaccessible to many people with physical or multiple disabilities. The inclusion of people with disabilities in exhibits or interpretation is still an area that many museums and historic sites could address. As the survey results from special education teachers indicate, some people still believe that museums are not places where all students are welcome because of noise or behavioral problems that students may cause. Through these seven key components for programs, the museum can construct learning centers for all audiences.

NOTES

1. The survey was distributed through the special-education@lists.teachers.net, teach-talk@lists.teachers.net, and tn-teachers@lists.teachers.net listservs. It was also posted on Face-book in the groups Tennessee Council for Exceptional Children, National Association of Special Education Teachers, and Special Education Resources for Kids; on LinkedIn in the Museum-Ed Group; and through Twitter. Postings to teacher discussion boards included History Teachers Discussion Board at http://www.schoolhistory.co.uk/forum/index.php and Teacher Forums—Teacher Chat at http://forums.theteacherscorner.net.

2. Results of the November 2, 2012, previsit survey sent to Rutherford County educators.

3. Sam Davis Home and Museum, "Educational Programs," http://www.samdavishome.org/education.php (accessed April 4, 2013).

4. From the March 2013 survey of the Sam Davis Home visit (in the author's possession).

5. From the March 2013 survey of the Sam Davis Home visit (in the author's possession).

Chapter Six

Conclusion

Successful museums continually grow and adapt to the world around them. From aristocratic beginnings in Western Europe for the wealthy, educated elite to community educational centers, museums have come a long way from the first exhibits of universities and world fairs. As today's museum reaches out to increasingly diverse audiences, engaging experiences for all visitors is essential. Museums and historic sites are more successful when they strive to implement universally designed and tactile education programs for all visitors, including those with accessibility or other special needs.

Most museums in the United States have tried to remove themselves from the early dime museums, sideshows, and other exhibitions that billed themselves as educational and entertaining experiences. Modern museum professionals replaced those displays, which exploited a variety of human beings, with exhibitions that tell the stories of people and places of the past through artifacts, spaces, and narratives. Moving forward, museum staff can use this manual to ensure that the exhibits and programs are fully inclusive for all audiences.

In 1990, the passage of the Americans with Disabilities Act (ADA) exemplified the move toward rights and inclusion in the workplace and the public for people of all abilities. The law ensured people with mobility issues access equal to that of any person, and while the ADA does not specifically address individuals with cognitive or intellectual delays, it did open the door to dialogue about all types of accessibility. As architects and designers reacted to the ADA, universal design was born and later adapted by museums.

Universal design, as a concept and in practice, benefits not only those with various accessibility or mobility issues but also the entire public. It might not be easy to make sure that every aspect of a building, exhibit, or program is up to universal design standards, but even the smallest changes can make a huge difference to visitors. Museum and historic site staff can start with ADA-required ramps and entrance and egress points, curb ramps, and adequate space for mobility assistance devices. Captions on introductory videos or Braille informational text are the next step. Then the museum can move forward with exhibit- and way-finding text, physical space dimensions, and the correct language for programs.

When museum educators pair universal design with object-centered learning in historic spaces, the result can be meaningful accessible programs. Although many consider universal design the ideal, museum staff can still create specific programs for various age-groups and abilities to enhance any particular group's experience onsite.

Even though large museums with seemingly infinite budgets and staff lead the way toward fully inclusive programs, small museums can learn from them and adapt programs that attract a variety of visitors. Large museums are leading the way, and in many cases art museums and children's museums have the most accessible programs for visitors. The inherent aspects of discovery and thought at these types of museums make the learning process more interactive and accessible to all ages and backgrounds.

The Museum Access Consortium (MAC) of New York City offers museum staff, volunteers, community members, and educators the opportunity to discuss strategy together and to develop successful programs. Other cities or regional areas can develop similar groups to meet occasionally and discuss success or strategies in education, access, and other museum issues. The access programs in New York City are so successful because of the partnership among a variety of people working together toward a common goal.

The Museum of Modern Art (MoMA) in New York is a great success story from the MAC; through community partnerships and focus groups, the "Meet Me at MoMA" program is one of the most successful ongoing educational programs for a specific population with special needs. The adults with dementia who visited MoMA were engaged in discussion and learned about the art while also interacting with other visitors and their companions. MoMA not only developed and regularly presents this program, but the museum website also offers guidelines for other museums to develop the program at museums around the world.

Another art museum making strides in inclusive educational programs for visitors with special needs, the Museum of Contemporary Art in Jacksonville, Florida, again shows that art museums lead the way for innovative programs at museums. The "Rainbow Artists" program for children with autism uses best practices to create educational and engaging activities. The activities not only teach the children about art but also increase communication, social relationships, and development while the student expresses him- or herself through a different medium of communication. Again, this museum makes materials available on its website for others to use and adapt.

Historic sites and museums offer different challenges from art museums. The New York City Transit Museum and the Lower East Side Tenement Museum took advantage of the unique stories and spaces that they occupy to create innovative programs for people with special needs. The Transit Museum recognized that a large part of its audience has an interest in the exhibits and subject matter and developed programs specifically for that audience. Children with autism now have a space to learn more about trains, transportation, technology, and history while communicating with other children, museum staff, and visitors. Additionally, the museum exemplifies working with the local community by offering real-world experiences and training for people with special needs by using their exhibits and museum space.

The Tenement Museum had the additional challenge of an inaccessible historic structure; the staff there used programs and special exhibits to give visitors with special needs an engaging experience outside of that historic space. Their future commitment to accessibility for all visitors is inspiring and should serve as an example to all other historic sites.

The Sam Davis Home case study shows that historic sites and museums offer students and visitors the unique opportunity to experience history and historic spaces and items firsthand. The case studies from the New York City Transit Museum, MoMA, and other large museums clearly indicated that visitors with intellectual disabilities can have an enriching experience at museums when educators combine effective exhibits and universal design environments with artifact based education techniques and inquiry methods of teaching. The model for programming at historic sites and museums meets the needs of people with intellectual disabilities and other cognitive or developmental delays. The model programs at larger museums and the case study from the Sam Davis Home show how successful universally designed and targeted programs can be. Even with small budgets and limited resources, staff and volunteers, in conjunction with community partners, can create meaningful opportunities for visitors with special needs.

This book encourages educators to follow the seven key elements of effective programs, presented in the previous chapter, to adapt their existing programs and create new learning experiences. These basic elements distill the basics of engaging and educational programs; the list is by no means comprehensive, and museum professionals should continue to add to and experiment with programming alternatives.

Customer service should be one of the main goals for any organization that serves the public, and sensitivity and awareness toward those individuals with special needs are always important. Museum staff are in the business of serving visitors just as they would any person who is offering a service. Training in techniques to communicate with all visitors, including those with sight, hearing, mobility issues, or other disabilities, is timely, especially because a significant portion of the population identifies as disabled in some way, and the number is increasing all the time because of aging baby boomers. A universally designed museum should include sensitivity and awareness in communication with all visitors to create a welcoming environment.

Sensitivity and awareness training should guide communication with visitors at the museum or on site, but staff should also converse regularly and efficiently with the community, other staff members, and teachers. Staff should work with members of the community in all stages of development for exhibits or programs, and this should always include people with disabilities. The employees and teachers or group leaders must also plan and communicate so that a visit to the museum or historic site is successful. The plan for the visit will almost inevitably change, so the staff should always be flexible and offer various opportunities for change and adaptation during the trip. Even though structure and flexibility are opposite attributes, museums and historic sites should make every effort to create programs that embody both characteristics.

Museums are most successful when they engage visitors through object-centered and inquiry-based sessions. This was apparent through the case study and model programs at larger museums, and smaller museums and historic sites benefit immensely from similar programs. Staff should strive to lead tours and programs with simple fixes, such as touch tables with excess or reproduction artifacts, visiting historic spaces, and allowing visitors to lead the tour with their own interests and questions. These tours and programs engage all visitors and create a learning experience that is more memorable and lasting; visitors with special needs benefit from this type of tour just as any other visitor would.

This book does not explore all of the options in this relatively new field of programs for people with special needs. There are many professionals at small museums and historic sites that create innovative and beneficial programs every day, and as the population becomes more aware of the growing population of individuals with disabilities, the field will continue to grow. The limited sample of programs and studies in this book serve instead only as a starting point for continued research and best practices in museum education. Once visitors feel welcomed at historic sites, museum staff can establish standards for programs based on those experiences.

Museums have changed exponentially throughout the years. Public historians today have the opportunity to enlarge and enhance museum audiences by creating effective, dynamic environments and programs such as the ones reviewed in this dissertation. Simply inviting groups of students with special needs to a historic site is not enough. Once the group is at the site, public historians must use their skills of engagement and belief in shared authority to help then teach social and life skills as well as provide educational experiences. The historic sites also offer the unique opportunity, in many cases, for students and visitors to see the historic structures and artifacts that people actually lived in or used in the past that they usually see only in history books. Firsthand experiences with the historic items can help students make those connections that make history and people from the past matter to them, and all visitors deserve to have that opportunity.

List of Appendices

Appendix A

Tenement Museum Language Processing Disorder Strategies

Appendix A

Language Processing Disorder: Strategies for Teaching Students with Special Needs

These Students Might	Teaching Tools	At the Tenement
• Have trouble distinguishing between words: hear "Listen here all of you, settle down quietly and stand in line" as "Histen ear olive you sit on down quietly nstandwin line."	• Familiarize students with any new vocabulary before the lesson.	• Introduce "tenement" and "immigrant" before delving into the context.
• Tune out quickly from a lecture-type presentation.	• Give written/pictorial directions to supplement verbal directions and underline the important terms.	• Write a timetable for the day's plans.
• Have difficulty listening when there is background noise.		• Use Venn diagrams/ spiderwebs to organize ideas.
	• Slow the rate of presentation and allow extra time for students to listen to, think about, and form their own thoughts.	• Make sure to include "buddy time" to allow time to "rehearse" answers.
• Need extra time to answer questions, need to rehearse statements, or need frequent reviews while learning new information.	• Omit nonessential details and double negatives.	• Focus on the stories of the people to keep it very concrete.
	• Avoid use of abstract language (metaphors, idioms, puns, etc.).	• "What can Natalie do?" as opposed to "If you were Natalie, what would you do?"
• Have difficulties understanding language concepts, making it difficult for them to integrate new ideas with prior knowledge.	• Utilize visual aids to supplement verbal information.	• Use the settings and photos in each apartment to tell the story through what kids see.

Appendix B

Tenement Museum Asperger's Syndrome Strategies

Asperger's Syndrome: Strategies for Teaching Students with Special Needs

These Students Might	Teaching Tools	At the Tenement
• Have difficulty reading social cues.	• Provide clear expectations and rules for behavior; don't expect them to know how to act.	• "At the Tenement Museum, we ask you to walk, not run, to listen when your classmates are talking and to raise your hand if you have a question."
• Have difficulty maintaining eye contact.	• Avoid "buddy time" when students must interact one on one.	• Rather than ask, "How would it feel to be on this boat?" ask, "What would have been hard about the boat ride I just described?"
• Have difficulty feeling empathy.	• Don't ask questions about "how would it feel?" Tell students how it would feel and focus questions around what students see; logical rather than emotional connections.	• Write an outline on the board at the beginning of each program and show students where in the program you are.
• Experience difficulty with transitions.	• Write a timetable for the day's plans.	• Be sure to close doors. Wait until after the Baldizzi recording ends to point out the elements of the room Josephine describes.
• Be affected by sensory stimuli.	• Use Venn diagrams/ spiderwebs to organize ideas. • Stay focused on the students in the room and the story at hand.	
• Stare off into space or doodle to help concentration.	• Don't be offended if the students aren't looking at you. It doesn't mean they aren't listening.	

Sam Davis Home Museum Scavenger Hunt

MEMORIAL AND REMEMBRANCE GALLERY

1. How did some of the artists decide what Sam looked like?
2. What vegetable was canned in Pulaski with the "Sam Davis" name on the label?

FARM AND FAMILY GALLERY

3. What plant is pictured on the walls? (major cash crop for the farm)
4. Name a toy that belonged to the Davis children. (Look in the case!)

RECOVERING THEIR STORY GALLERY

5. What is special about the tiny blue bead in the cabin window?
6. What job did Gracey Davis do?

BEYOND THE WAR GALLERY

7. What is the name of the type of carriage on display?

CIVIL WAR IN MIDDLE TENNESSEE GALLERY

8. How many amputations took place on federal troops during the Civil War?

9. Name three battles in which the 1st Tennessee Volunteers took part.

SAM DAVIS GALLERY

10. What made the Spencer rifle more effective than those in the first gallery?

Appendix D

Sam Davis Home
"Life under the Gun" Script

LIFE OF A SOLDIER

1. Introduction

    a. Ask if students have seen a Civil War movie or battle flick or read books
    b. Soldiers from both the North and South shared many things in common
    c. Reasons soldiers joined the army:

    - Excitement
    - Patriotism (states' rights/save the Union)
    - Peer pressure
    - Protect home and family

2. Describe uniforms

    a. Shell jacket/sack coat
    b. Pants
    c. Shoes
    d. Shirts
    e. Hat/kepi

3. Describe equipment

    a. Rifle

      b. Cartridge box
      c. Cap pouch
      d. Canteen
      e. Haversack
      f. Blanket roll

4. Weapons and their usage

      a. Rifle
      b. Bayonet
      c. Revolver
      d. Bowie knife
      e. Sword
      f. Derringer

5. Contents of haversacks

      a. Food

            a. Pork
            b. Beef
            c. Vegetables (fresh and desiccated)
            d. Bread

      b. Utensils

            a. Cup, mug, and musket
            b. Skillet
            c. Plate
            d. Canteen (mess kit)
            e. Knife, fork, and spoon

      c. Personal hygiene

            a. Toothbrush
            b. Comb
            c. Razor
            d. Soap

      d. Entertainment

            a. Cards
            b. Dominoes

    c. Books/papers/letters

- Bible (prayer books)
- Pencil and paper

e. Games

    a. Baseball
    b. Wrestling
    c. Racing
    d. Poppin' lice
    e. Snow (snowmen, ramparts, snowball fights, etc.)

Appendix E

Sam Davis Home "Seasons on the Farm" Script

SEASONS ON THE FARM SCAVENGER HUNT

Objective: Children will discover various seasonal chores on the Davis's nineteenth-century farm.

- Please note there are two sides to the scavenger hunt—one for younger grades 1–4, one for grades 5–8. The hunt for older children includes directional clues so they will have to rely on their property map to find the locations (this side is labeled 5–8).

Ask the children if they've ever been on a scavenger hunt. Explain to them that historians are kind of like detectives in the way they piece together clues from the past to answer questions about our history. They will be reading clues to learn more about specific jobs that people had on a nineteenth-century farm in Middle Tennessee.

Directions:

- Divide children into five groups (for younger children, one chaperone needs to accompany each group of children).
- Each group will receive one clipboard with a property map, answer sheet, and pencil. (Make sure they have the grade-appropriate clipboard!)
- Each clipboard has a clue on the back. The color of your clue is your "team color." Explain to the children that when they go from each location, they will be reading *only* their color clue.

- Show them the property map on their clipboard. Explain to them that they are starting at the *museum*.
- For older grades, emphasize the importance of the map. They will have to use their compass rose to find locations on the map.
- Also explain that no clues are located outside of the fence line in the backyard or past the road.
- Rules for the groups:

  - No running.
  - Stay with your group—work together!
  - It is not a race to finish—finding the correct answer is more important than finishing first.
  - When you complete all eight questions, return to the veranda.

Suggested Readings

These sources here will help museums create inclusive and accessible exhibitions and spaces. The literature is still developing, but these sources are a wonderful start.

BOOKS

American Association of People with Disabilities and the Employment Practices and Measurement Rehabilitation Research Training Center at the University of New Hampshire. *2011 Annual Disability Statistics Compendium*. Durham: University of New Hampshire Institute on Disability, 2011.

Black, Graham. *The Engaging Museum: Developing Museums for Visitor Involvement*. New York: Routledge, 2005.

Dana, John Cotton. *The New Museum. Selected Writings*. Newark, NJ: Newark Museum Association, 1999.

Davis, Elaine. *How Students Understand the Past: From Theory to Practice*. Walnut Creek, CA: AltaMira Press, 2005.

Garland-Thomson, Rosemarie. *Extraordinary Bodies: Figuring Physical Disability in American Culture and Literature*. New York: Columbia University Press, 1997.

Harpers Ferry Center Accessibility Task Force. *Special Populations: Programmatic Accessibility Guidelines*. Harpers Ferry, WV: National Park Service, June 1999.

International Council of Museums. *Running a Museum: A Practical Handbook*. Paris: International Council of Museums, 2010.

Kaufman, James M., and Daniel P. Hallahan. *Special Education: What It Is and Why We Need It*. Boston: Pearson, 2005.

Lord, Barry, ed. *The Manual of Museum Learning*. Lanham, MD: AltaMira Press, 2007.

Majewski, Janice. *Part of Your General Public Is Disabled: A Handbook for Guides in Museums, Zoos, and Historic Houses*. Washington, DC: Smithsonian Institution Press, 1987.

Nielson, Kim E. *A Disability History of the United States*. New York: Beacon Press, 2012.

Office of Special Education Programs. *Twenty-Five Years of Progress in Educating Children with Disabilities through IDEA*. Washington, DC: U.S. Department of Education, 2007.

Playforth, Sarah. Resource Disability Portfolio series. London: Council for Museums, Archives & Libraries, 2003.

Sandell, Richard, ed. *Museums, Society, Inequality (Museum Meanings)*. New York: Routledge, 2002.

Sandell, Richard, Jocelyn Dodd, and Rosemarie Garland-Thomson. *Re-Presenting Disability: Activism and Agency in the Museum.* London: Routledge, 2010.
Sherman, Daniel J. *Museums and Difference.* Bloomington: Indiana University Press, 2008.
Shorter, Edward. *The Kennedy Family and the Story of Mental Retardation.* Philadelphia: Temple University Press, 2000.

ARTICLES, CHAPTERS, AND OTHER SHORT PUBLISHED WORKS

Addis, Michela. "New Technologies and Cultural Consumption: Edutainment Is Born!" *European Journal of Marketing* 39 (2005): 729–36.
Americans with Disabilities Act of 1990, Public Law 101-336, 101st Cong., 2nd sess. (July 26, 1990), 104 Stat. 327.
Barbour, Erwin H. "Museums and the People." *Publications of the Nebraska Academy of Sciences* 8 (1912): 1–12.
Blandy, Doug. "Community-Based Lifelong Learning in Art for Adults with Mental Retardation: A Rationale, Conceptual Foundation, and Supportive Environments." *Studies in Art Education* 34 (Spring 1993): 167–75.
Burch, Susan, and Katherine Ott, eds. "Disability and the Practice of Public History." Special issue, *Public Historian* 27 (Spring 2005).
Delin, Annie. "Buried in the Footnotes: The Absence of Disabled People in the Collective Imagery of Our Past." In *Museums, Society, and Inequality (Museum Meanings)*, edited by Richard Sandell, 84–97. New York: Routledge, 2002.
Godkin, Edwin L. "A Word about Museums." *The Nation*, July 27, 1865, 113–14.
Goode, George Brown. "The Relationships and Responsibilities of Museums." *Science* 2 (1895): 197–209.
Kennedy, John F. "Special Message to the Congress on Education." February 6, 1962. Gerhard Peters and John T. Woolley, eds., *The American Presidency Project.* http://www.presidency.ucsb.edu/ws/?pid=8858 (accessed February 24, 2013).
———. "Special Message to the Congress on Mental Illness and Mental Retardation." February 5, 1963. Gerhard Peters and John T. Woolley, eds., *The American Presidency Project.* http://www.presidency.ucsb.edu/ws/?pid=9546 (accessed February 24, 2013).
Lepouras, George, and Costas Vassilakis. "Virtual Museums for All: Employing Game Technology for Edutainment." *Virtual Reality* 8 (2005): 96–106.
Mayerson, Arlene. "The History of the ADA: A Movement Perspective." *Disability Rights Education and Defense Fund*, 1992. http://dredf.org/publications/ada_history.shtml (accessed January 10, 2013).
Sandell, Richard, Annie Delin, Jocelyn Dodd, and Jackie Gay. "In the Shadow of the Freakshow: The Impact of Freakshow Tradition on the Display and Understanding of Disability History in Museums." *Disability Studies Quarterly* 25 (Fall 2005). http://dsq-sds.org/article/view/614/791.
Stephens, Elizabeth. "Twenty-First Century Freak Show: Recent Transformations in the Exhibition of Non-Normative Bodies." *Disability Quarterly Studies* 25 (Summer 2005): 1–12.
Woollard, Vicky. "Caring for the Visitor." In *Running a Museum: A Practical Handbook*, edited by the International Council of Museums, 105–18. Paris: International Council of Museums, 2010.

WEBSITES

Association of Science-Technology Centers. "Resource Center: Accessible Practices: Museums' Legal Obligations." http://www.astc.org/resource/access (accessed March 1, 2012).
Cohen, Judith. "Etiquette." *Community Resources for Independence.* http://www.crinet.org/education/Independent%20Living/Etiquette (accessed March 4, 2012).

Department of Justice. "ADA Requirements for Small Towns." U.S. Department of Justice, 2000. http://www.ada.gov/smtown.htm#anchor15334 (accessed January 13, 2013).

Department of Justice, Disability Rights Section. "Maintaining Accessibility in Museums." http://www.ada.gov/business/museum_access.htm (accessed November 29, 2012).

Disability Resource Agency for Independent Living. "Disability Awareness Sensitivity Training Presentation." http://www.cfilc.org/.../Disability%20Awareness%20Sensitivity%20 (accessed March 2012).

"Expanding the Concept of Universal Design." http://www.universaldesign.com (accessed April 4, 2013).

John F. Kennedy Presidential Library. "JFK and People with Intellectual Disabilities." http://www.jfklibrary.org/JFK/JFK-in-History/JFK-and-People-with-Intellectual-Disabilities.aspx (accessed February 24, 2013).

Museum Access Consortium. "What Is the Museum Access Consortium (MAC)?" *Museum Access Consortium*. http://www.cityaccessny.org/mac.php (accessed April 30, 2012).

Index